Rivers of Gold

Robert J. Brown

Copyright © Robert J. Brown 2006
All rights reserved

Email : robert@robertjbrown.co.uk
Website : www.robertjbrown.co.uk

Acknowledgements

Thanks to those who read and gave encouragement: Lorna Smout, Richard Lindsay and Stephen Coleman.

Thanks to Gary Cook a travelling companion beyond compare.

And to my wife Melanie, a woman in a million.

Thanks also to Kanoe People and Up North Adventures of Whitehorse for help with the logistics, without which our journey would not have been possible. See their websites at www.kanoepeople.com and www.upnorth.yk.ca

Photo credits - front and back cover, Gary Cook. For more of his images see his website at www.garycook.co.uk

For Buster, the greatest of dogs and a wonderful friend.

Prelude

A thin crust of ice fell away from the flysheet of the tent as I opened the zip, coating my sleeping bag-warm forearm in biting fragments. I pulled my boots on without tying the laces and stood up into the dawn. The sun was struggling this late August morning. It was a pale and haloed spectre, barely managing to throw light through a swirling grey wall of fog. Dressed in a woolly hat, T-shirt and long johns I sprinted over to where we had stashed our gear, my laces whipping around my ankles like angry snakes.

With fingers already turning into uncooperative sausages I unscrewed the lid of the plastic barrel containing my outer clothing. My fleeces, trousers, coat and gloves had been put in here before going to bed last night in case I had spilled any food, or wiped greasy hands on them and thereby turned them inadvertently into bear magnets. This was bear country. We were camped in the woods at Lower Laberge at the northern (downstream) end of Lake Laberge, Yukon Territory. We had yet to see a bear, but we knew that they were about and sharing the woods with creatures bigger and potentially higher on the food chain than us prevented even the most mundane tasks, such as getting dressed, from becoming boring

Around me the silence was intense. There was no wind and the mist moved under its own volition. High above me the sky was slowly brightening with the faintest hint of blue as the strengthening sun promised to burn away the landscape's overnight shroud. As I shrugged into my clothes I could hear Gary getting up behind me, then his size elevens pounded over. "Jesus Christ, it's freezing," he needlessly informed me.

"Fancy a brew while we wait for the fog to burn off?" I asked.

"Ahh, yeah," Gary replied, as he tried to get into his trousers without putting his stocking feet down amongst the dew and the frost.

This was our fourth day on the Yukon River. We had rented a canoe in Whitehorse and we were headed to Dawson, 460miles from our starting point. The first day had seen us enter Lake Laberge, a huge body of water 30miles long and 1.25miles wide at its narrowest point. Whilst the Yukon had had a swift current, making canoeing easy, the lake was like the sea, except that there wasn't even a tide we could make use of. But the water wasn't still. Menacingly malevolent would be one way to describe it, even on a still day. We had edged along the eastern shore, feeling rather like Roman explorers, not daring to leave the guidance of the beach lest the waves become unmanageable, or we simply came to the edge of the world and fell off.

Part way through our second day on the lake the wind had got up and when two consecutive waves had spilled over the bow and into the boat we had made for shore to lay up. We had erected a shelter beneath a benevolent pine as a bracing horizontal rain had begun to fall and we fully expected to be land-bound for the rest of the day, though typically for this part of the world within an hour the weather had totally changed again. We had finally reached the abandoned settlement of Lower Laberge in time to relax in the golden light of a glorious sunset.

As the camping stove hissed underneath a pot of water in the strengthening dawn I ambled down to the river's edge. I watched the Yukon's water spill out from the lake to resume its long journey to the sea. On the opposite bank the pines stood silent sentinel, their ragged tops clawing up from the vaporous grey air hanging over the water. A squirrel yelled a machine gun chatter from somewhere behind me, shattering the silence as surely as if a bomb had gone off. A flotilla of mergansers darted forward noisily across the river like tiny multicoloured jet skis. They stopped suddenly in unison, then raced forward again in some unknowable avian game.

Whilst I watched the racing current in the river the water in the pot had boiled and Gary handed me a cup of steaming tea. I held it gratefully in both hands, its heat coming through the plastic and my Thinsulate gloves to warm my fingers, blissful. Such simple pleasures. As I stood there with my tea exhaling steam into the frigid air a wolf's howl cut through the forest. The resonance of the note passed through me causing the hair on my arms and neck to stand up. The cry was joined by, what sounded like, two others. I was spellbound; the plaintive notes all consuming. A surge of an unexpected and unknown emotion seemed to fill my chest and lift my soul. I grinned inanely at Gary who was similarly transfixed. The howls died into a series of yelps and then the silence returned. It was my first brush with a live wolf and I was elated. I felt deliriously alive and my veins fizzed with Champagne. The call of the wild had struck a powerful chord. My love affair with the far north had begun.

Chapter One

Finally we stood on the shores of the Teslin River at the roadhouse settlement of Johnson's Crossing. Seven years had passed since we had last been alongside a Yukon Territory river and over half of the current day had already passed. We would be taking it easy on a short afternoon paddle just to get us back into the swing of it. The Alaska Highway Bridge towered above us; a sign of civilization, which repelled me as surely as the wilderness beckoning on our left pulled me. Our plan was to follow the Teslin for 120 miles until its waters mingled with those of the Yukon at the abandoned settlement of Hootalinqua. We would then re-acquaint ourselves with the 110 miles of the Yukon between Hootalinqua and Carmacks, a section of the 460-mile journey we had undertaken in 1997. We would then hop on a bus to Dawson and from there, hire a car to drive up the Dempster Highway to the Arctic Circle. I was practically quivering with anticipation.

The truck that had dropped us off turned a wide arc in the dirt and rumbled off back up the steep hill to the highway, leaving us in its dusty wake. We began reorganizing our stuff, removing food from rucksacks and putting it into the waterproof and bear-proof barrels. Whilst Gary tried to make sure that the things we would need first were at the top of the barrels I headed back up to the roadhouse to fill our five-litre water bladder and our individual one-litre water bottles.

This was the last chance saloon. Once we set off we would have no contact with the outside world and would be enveloped by the forest. For the next eight days on the river our survival was to be entirely our responsibility. If we had forgotten anything it would be tough; I had awoken from a dream on the plane from London to Vancouver sweating in a panic that we had set off without a tin opener, or matches to light a fire and the gas stove.

At the roadhouse I asked if there was somewhere I could fill up our water bottles and was told that there was a faucet outside. I went around the side of the building and the only tap I could find had a huge length of hosepipe attached to it. I couldn't figure out how to undo the clip on the tap without breaking something, so I just pushed the tip of the hose into the water bladder. As the water swirled in I briefly envisaged being poisoned by some bug-killing chemical that had been mixed in a watering can with the end of the hose.

Suitably replete with water of dubious quality I bought two muffins and then waddled back down to the river under the weight of my load. Gary had finished the reorganizing when I got there and we sat on the ground and ate the muffins. A mosquito lanced into my forearm in what I hoped wasn't a portent of things to come.

We packed our gear into the canoe under a grey sky and pushed out into what for us, was the unknown. The Teslin River is a tributary of the Yukon. Its source is high in the mountains of British Columbia, but it doesn't travel far before it is entrapped in Teslin Lake. The lake snakes over the border into Yukon Territory, finally spitting out the river once more just in front of the Alaska Highway and the bridge here at Johnson's Crossing. The river heads north following the western edge of the Big Salmon Range of mountains, almost parallel to the Yukon.

Of course, it's the Yukon River that everyone has heard of, in part because it is a vast artery of North America, travelling some 2300 miles into the Bering Sea and in part because of its role as a highway in the Klondike Gold Rush of 1898. Just as the Yukon, the Teslin was an important highway to early settlers. It's likely that the river's first explorers were the First Nation tribe (in Canada the indigenous people are referred to as First Nation people rather than Indians) of the Tlinget, who had settled on Teslin Lake, in the 18th century. As their population expanded down-river they were met by the Chilkat tribes expanding upwards from coastal Alaska. The Chilkat people were the foremost traders on the upper Yukon and they were exploiting new areas for fur trapping, the products of which could be sent down-river and eventually sold on to the likes of the Hudson's Bay Company. Eventually, by the 1870's the first Europeans had begun to push into the area prospecting for gold. During the Klondike Gold Rush of 1898 and the years that followed, the Teslin was used by some as an alternative route to the Dawson goldfields and some river traffic existed to supply the smaller goldfield of Livingston in the early 1900's. However, the Teslin was always a comparative backwater compared to the bustling Yukon and Klondike rivers and by the 1940's with new roads built and gold all but exhausted, the last residents on the river had left and the Teslin reverted to its pre-goldrush, wilderness state.

As we took our first paddle strokes very quickly the river fanned out from the pinch point that the Alaska Highway Bridge had exploited. The hills receded, cloaked in low lying cloud and the riverbanks became flat and fringed with tall lush grasses and willows, indicating the presence of marshes and backwater sloughs. Beyond the grass the pines cowered, unwilling to get their feet wet, but jostling each other forward so that the occasional member of the vanguard would be forced into the marsh and topple over.

Very quickly my mind adjusted to a new reality. Although I am by no means a city dweller (I come from a small town in the north east of England, on the urban fringe) my life is busy with my wife and friends, a job, computers, telephones, cars, faxes, television, football matches, the gym and all the other paraphernalia of a western life. Now I was sloughing off 'civilization' and my priorities were changing to suit these new surroundings. My senses were awakened and my ears especially were underwhelmed. With no background noise such as the drone of traffic, or the hum of a refrigerator, or a computer fan, any noise was joltingly clear. Underneath a glowering sky I was acutely aware of the weather from which there would be no escape; we would live outdoors for the next three weeks.

I was alive with the possibilities of adventure. There could be encounters with animals of great beauty such as wolves, or bears, or eagles, encounters that had an element of danger. We would certainly see some spectacular scenery and we would be responsible for our own survival within it. We might have to cope with rapids and with harsh weather and with the plain old unexpected.

For now the river's current was disappointingly lazy and our forward progress could hardly be detected by watching the passing shoreline. Instead I looked into the crystal clear water and watched the rocks of the riverbed go by. A light rain began to fall and the impacting raindrops obscured my watery odometer and filled the air with a gentle static.

Our canoe was the type of vessel shaped like those birch bark canoes that people associate with the American Indians. It was a model known as an Old Town Canoe, some seventeen feet in length with a seat front and back for the passengers to sit on. Propulsion comes from single bladed paddles held with one hand on top gripping a small T of plastic. Birch bark had been replaced in the hull by very tough plastic. However, I now noticed, rather disconcertingly, that there was quite a large crack in the hull below the waterline. There was no sign of a leak thanks to a double skinned hull, but I mentally vowed to keep an eye on it and tried to remember where we had stashed the duct tape for just such repairs.

The river was extremely shallow in places and several times in the first hour our paddles hit the riverbed and our hull scraped alarmingly over the gravel. Long streamers of water weeds grasped at our paddles and caressed the bottom of the canoe. Although I was warm enough paddling, the air had a chill to it, despite it still being August, a month which at home could be the hottest time of the year. The summer here was already waning and becoming a memory. The aspens, birch, cottonwoods and willows amongst the pines were tinged with yellow and gold. This was a land turning towards winter.

I was disappointed to see log cabins amongst the trees during those early miles. They were a sign of the human race that I was hoping to leave behind. Gradually though they became less in number as the distance from the access point of the highway increased. The rain stopped and slowly the hills closed in, increasing the gloom of the gathering evening. The hillsides were thickly hirsute with coniferous timber and the woods enveloped us in their dark embrace. The river was forced into a narrower, deeper, faster flowing channel and we could relax a little and still keep up momentum.

A raven flew over us letting out a loud rolling 'krooonk' as it approached. A moment later the crisp echo of the call came back to us from the woods ahead. I marvelled at the beauty of the raven and at the clarity of the air. The bird halted its rhythmic flight momentarily and pulled its wings in slightly as it came over us. It dipped in the air and the slipstream over its back sucked up a solitary feather between its shoulders. The feather fluttered momentarily before finding its place back amongst its anthracite neighbours. The raven tilted its head so that a black shiny eye could investigate the interlopers below. Satisfied, it flexed its wings and continued onwards, the silence rushing back in its wake.

Up ahead I spotted the incongruous splash of white in a tree, which gave away the presence of a bald eagle. It was sat on a branch overhanging the river on the right hand bank. We hastily reached for our cameras, which had been stored in bags at our feet for the duration of the rain showers. I have a twenty year old Pentax ME Super which has seen action on four continents and has had two repairs. It is a great piece of equipment and I have a three-hundred millimetre lens to attach to it for shooting wildlife. Its age means that it still requires something called 'film', and so you can't see your photos until they have been 'developed'. Gary has a Fuji Finepix SLR camera, which was great because with a digital we could look at photos each night in camp. Suitably armed with cameras around necks, we pulled towards shore and lined up parallel with the bank and then brought in our paddles and drifted towards the eagle.

We started shooting early, unsure of how close we would get before the eagle took off. Between shots I watched intently, looking for the tell-tale dip that the bird's head would make the instant before it opened its wings to fly. It didn't come. We held our breaths as we cruised right under it. It watched us intently from an altitude of about ten feet. From a distance the eagle had looked magnificent, but up close the illusion was tarnished. It looked slightly bedraggled, the white feathers of its head were mussed, giving the impression it had been dragged through a hedge backwards and straggles of white down poked out through the brown of its breast. It was nevertheless, an awe-inspiring creature. The yellow toes gripping the tree branch were tipped with fearsome daggers and the bird's beak was an evilly curved scimitar. Its eyes were something else. The cornea was bright and crystal clear, reflecting the light in a shining pinprick and below it was a yellow iris and black pupil. A brow ridge covered the eye giving the bird a stern look. It swivelled its head to follow us. Only when we were some twenty feet beyond its perch did the bird dip and take off. The wings expanded to their full seven-foot span and they stroked languidly at the air making a sound like the whooshing of successive firework rocket launches.

It wasn't long after seeing the eagle that we began to look for somewhere to camp. Gary was sat behind me with the relevant map page of our river guide open under a clear plastic bag. We were following Gus Karpes' excellent guides, 'The Teslin River' and 'Exploring the Upper Yukon River', which not only had maps, but also information on the history of the area. As is usual on our trips Gary had taken on the role of navigator, carefully watching the landscape roll by and marking progress on the map. Up ahead on the left, just after the river narrowed, was Squanga Creek and on the Right Bank, immediately before that, the map showed a possible camping spot near an abandoned cabin. We pulled up against the right hand shore and hopped out using convenient rocks as stepping-stones so that we didn't get our feet wet.

"Hello bear!" we called in unison and clapped our hands.

Our hand claps sounded like rifle shots and raced around the woods shattering the peace. I almost winced at the noise we made. The silence had been so profound that in the cathedral of the woods a clap felt like sacrilege. Still, better to disturb the peace than startle a bear and end up seeing one from the inside.

I held onto the rope on the prow of the canoe whilst Gary had a quick look around. We needed somewhere where there was enough space and flat ground between the trees to squeeze the tent. We also needed somewhere not too far from the tent where we could have a fire. Within a minute Gary was back shaking his head.

"No good, but I think we may be just short of the campsite marked on the map. Let's just walk along a bit," he said.

Gary walked ahead while I escorted the boat by its lead. It was a bit awkward as protruding rocks would catch the prow and I would have to try to jiggle it free. In several places the rocky nature of the riverbank gave way to thick mud, which I tried to skip around, moving further from the boat and making it all the harder to steer. It was during this hopscotch advance that I spotted a print in the mud. It was a perfect wolf print. Its edges were pin sharp and it had sunk to quite a depth. It was a heavy animal and it had big feet. I have a German shepherd dog and this print dwarfed any track my dog would make. We stood and looked at that print for several minutes, thinking about the animal and what it represented. We were on our own in the wilderness. And this truly was a wilderness.

In Britain we don't have anywhere wild. I mean, people talk about such and such an area of the Highlands or the far north of Scotland as being Britain's last true wilderness, but it isn't really wild. For me the wolf and the bear are the wilderness and if they have been removed from a landscape, then that landscape is no longer wild. It is rather like a film set, in that it looks the part, but it's merely a hollow shell.

Tingling with a sense of excitement at the possibility of seeing a wolf we continued on. We found the promised camping spot, but the presence of the old cabin ruined it for us. We didn't want to camp by the signs of human activity. We got back into the canoe and crossed over to the other side of the river. Immediately downstream of the mouth of Squanga Creek we found a perfect camp.

A gently sloping pebbly beach gave way to the forest floor. The scaly pillars of pines were surrounded by a green carpet of a light green feathery plant that I couldn't recognise. Several trails led off into the woods, their surface brown, dry and compacted and veined with tree roots. My hiking boots felt some give in the ground and it resonated with the distinctive hollow clump I have come to associate with walking in a coniferous forest.

It didn't take long to get the gear unloaded and the tent set up. There was already a circle of stones in a small clearing, which contained the remains of someone else's fire. We spent a few minutes gathering deadwood for our own campfire.

Obviously our campground had been used before, as had several of the places we would find, as canoeists tend to travel at similar speeds and there are only so many suitable places available, but the sign of previous visitors did nothing to quell our sense of adventure. We knew that we weren't the first explorers here, but that didn't matter; it was new territory to us.

Although the rain had stopped, at first the fire struggled. I looked around again, this time further afield, clapping nervously as I went, in the hopes of finding something really old and dry beneath a tree. What I found were some spruce branches that some moron had recently torn off a perfectly good tree. Unfortunately, not everyone has the brains not to damage or fell trees when there is plenty of dead wood if you only make the effort to look for it.

I picked up the spruce and took it back to our sputtering fire.

"This'll get it going," I said to Gary.

"It's still green," he said, with a look that said 'pillock'.

"I know. Watch this though," I said, laying the boughs over the fire.

At first nothing happened and Gary's expression turned to a sceptical 'dumb ass'. But gradually the weak flames sputtering beneath the spruce bough finally warmed the needles up to a critical point. There was a brief 'sssss' and then the needles exploded into a crackling flame that shot up a foot and a half and set my eyebrows curling. I lurched back from the flame as Gary's expression transmogrified into a high eyebrow, round mouthed, 'bloody hell.'

"That is why forest fires in a coniferous wood are really, really bad news," I said with a didactic air of authority.

A bus driver in Whitehorse had told us that this summer there had been several fires that had raged out of control in the Yukon Territory, devouring around 1.8million hectares of land. Smoke had still been a visible blue smudge on the horizon when we had landed at the airport. I had come across the fire-lighting qualities of spruce in my career as a countryside ranger. One of the sites I manage is an ancient semi-natural woodland. It's deciduous, with wych elm and ash making up the majority of the canopy, but every January it is unfortunate that a minority of people think that it's okay to dispose of their Christmas trees by pitching them over the fence into the wood. This adds to the Leylandii hedge clippings that other similarly minded folk have been pitching in there all summer. Rather than allowing all this effluvia to build up causing a visual nuisance, suppressing the ground flora, and providing fire-starters for the resident miscreant youths, I burn it off whilst I'm burning brashings from the tree operations I do as routine. Spruce Christmas trees and Leylandii go up like a bomb thanks to their resinous sap. If your fire is struggling to start, whack on a spruce.

We ate our evening meal sat on logs beside the fire as a light drizzle again began to filter down through the trees. The heat from the fire was such that whilst wearing a hat it was almost possible to believe that it wasn't raining at all, but then there was a loud rumble of thunder.

I took the pots down to the river to wash up, wanting to get that chore done before a thunderstorm got going. I filled the cooking pans with river water to soak for a minute whilst I rinsed off the plates with a scouring pad. It only took a few minutes to do the necessary but by then my fingers were freezing. Still on the gravel of the riverbank I sat back on my haunches with my hands in my armpits to try to get some circulation back. The sky above me felt vast and the river stretched away to infinity to my left and right. Even though the wooded hillsides prevented me seeing very far to my front and rear I could sense the immensity of the forest and I felt truly insignificant. Whilst we had been eating the world had been reduced to that small circle of warmth and radiance around the fire, but now that sense of security, of being the centre of the universe, was gone. I was suddenly aware that I hadn't made any noise for several minutes and although the smoke from the campfire behind me was advertising my presence to the bears I began to feel a bit exposed.

I stood up and clapped, chasing away the bears in my mind. Rationally, I knew that I was safer here than at home, but the neurones in my primitive brainstem were bleeping like Sigourney Weaver's life-form detector in the film 'Aliens'. When I had told friends and colleagues back home what Gary and I were intending to do for our summer holidays, many of them had thought I was mad, or they declared how fantastic it would be, but that they wouldn't have the courage to do it. 'Too risky'. 'Bears will kill your ass'. Odd reactions I thought. Our sense of what constitutes a risk seems to be way off kilter. There were twenty fatalities due to bears in Alaska between 1900 and 1985. That's roughly one fatality every four years. In the paltry ten years between 1975 and 1985, nineteen Alaskans were killed by domestic dogs. That's almost two a year and yet perplexingly we are happy to share our homes, me included, with these savage killing machines.

Being killed by a wild animal in these days of human dominance and supremacy is such a rarity that it provokes reactions of horror, which are totally out of proportion. As I write, an unfortunate teenage surfer has just been killed by a sixteen-foot great white shark off Adelaide, Australia. It made the national newspapers here and the evening television news. Predictably and depressingly boats are now out to kill every big great white in the vicinity, as if sharks have no right to be predators in the ocean where we might want to go every now and again to flop around doing passable impressions of shark food. It makes no sense to kill the shark involved let alone to kill every shark nearby. Imagine a mugger who kills a pedestrian. Witnesses describe the attacker as a white male, aged 18-30. The police go out and kill every white male aged 18-30 within a twenty mile radius (in my imaginary scenario there is a death penalty for murder, so this makes perfect sense).

Man made fatalities on the other hand, other than homicide, are just shrugged off or ignored, no matter how frequently they occur. Such is the case with our favourite death trap, the car. Every day I drive to work and every day, without fail, the traffic report on the radio announces the hold ups on the main arterial routes due to crashes. Knowing that there will be an inevitable crash doesn't stop me, or anyone else, getting into a car. Neither does the fact that on average ten people will die that day on Britain's roads. Outside in the Yukon's forests there are no car crashes, no muggers, no violent drunks, no dangerous machines or industrial accidents and logic tells me that I'm far safer here than at home.

I picked up the pots, plates and cutlery and headed back into the trees. A squirrel scolded me as I passed and the trees shivered slightly as the rain became harder though the thunder seemed mercifully to have ceased. I rejoined Gary by the warmth of the fire. I have known Gary since we were about six years old when his parents moved into the house next door-but-one to mine. Though there is only nine months between our ages, because of the way our birthdays fall he was in the year above me at school.

Growing up we were always outside. We would play out on the street with other kids, playing football and hide-and-seek and tear-about games we had made up. We would stay out until our parents were forced to come out and call us in. As the summer dusk fell the blackbirds would be singing their throaty melodies, marking out their territories or wooing their mates in the gardens around us. They would shout their clattering alarms as we hid and sought amongst the bushes or frightened them from cover with carelessly aimed footballs. The calls of blackbirds as evenings draw in always remind me of my childhood.

As we got older we would camp out in Gary's back garden in his father's old tent. The evening would start with a bonfire on which we would burn toast on sticks or char potatoes wrapped in tin foil, serenaded all the time by the blackbirds. As darkness gathered we would retreat to the tent amongst six small apple trees. Sleep was a state difficult to achieve. The tent had a separate groundsheet so that as we lay down we could see the grass outside. I cringed at the scurrying movement of the centipedes and huge black ground beetles that occasionally blundered into the tent, though even then, I was aware that to kill them for trespass, as many kids would have done, was more than harsh. After all, the space beneath the apple trees wasn't our home. I remember being woken up by the snuffling of a hedgehog outside and then lying awake listening to the rustle of the leaves in the breeze and the occasional 'keewick' of a tawny owl.

As our sense of adventure outgrew the confines of the garden we would explore the local woods and we found ourselves cycling five miles or so to the banks of the river Leven, a tributary of the Tees. The woods along the Leven drew us like iron fillings to a magnet. We would make dens and explore with pencil and paper, making maps and naming streams and gullies like explorers in a new land. One summer day in particular is etched in my memory.

We were slowly walking up the bed of a stream. The water was clear and ankle deep, pushing coldly against the rubber of my wellingtons. We stumbled alternately over gravel riffles and through pools bedded with cloying mud. I enjoyed stopping for a few moments in such pools watching the brown mud billow around my feet to be gently removed like scudding clouds by the current. I would slowly settle into the substrate as the water cleared. Anchored this way into the very skin of the landscape I would watch fascinated, at the antics of stream skaters in the pools. These slender black insects darted hurriedly out from the banks, gliding over the surface on long water repellent legs to attack other insects that had blundered into the trap made by the physics of surface tension. A few minutes later we struggled to move as we battled free of the mud.

The earthen banks of the gully held us in a damp and shadowy world decorated with dangling tree roots and clinging ferns. High above us the trees loomed, filtering the sun through their verdant canopy, their trunks darkened with glossy ivy. As we moved up the stream the ravine we were in shallowed until the top was at head height. Something, a tiny movement or just an awareness of a presence, made me look up and I was frozen. There, barely ten feet away was a female roe deer. She stood stock still, looking right at me. She was in a shaft of sunlight that had somehow penetrated the leafy roof above. I could see the bristly looking hairs that made up the creature's coat. Her eyes were huge and soft, her nose a wet glossy black that was momentarily hidden by a flicking tongue. The two velvet trumpets she used as ears moved towards me to pick up the sound of my heartbeat, which was threatening to burst out through my own eardrums. I could sense that Gary, slightly behind me, had seen the deer at the same time as me, for there was no more motion or sound from him.

Time stood still and the only movement were the midges dancing in the warm sun above the deer, their wings blurred into golden halos around their tiny bodies. Then in an almost silent explosion the deer was gone, though not forgotten. Before that moment and ever since wildlife has been a source of increasing amazement to me. At the age of twelve, David Attenborough's series 'Life on Earth' was released on British television. It was an epic tale of evolution and showed the stunning variety of the natural world today. I was spellbound and that single event in my life had a profound affect. I went on to study Zoology at university and I subsequently, in a roundabout way, became a countryside ranger. Here I am, at the age of thirty-nine, still turning over stones to see what crawls out from beneath them like a ten year old boy.

Chapter Two

Inside the tent it was light enough to read the dial of my watch. Five-thirty am. The silence was odd, not because there were no human sounds, but because there was no avian dawn chorus. Back home a woodland dawn would have been saturated in birdsong, but here nothing stirred. Just as I was thinking that perhaps life on earth had died out overnight a ubiquitous squirrel chattered. I could faintly hear its tiny clawed toes tapping and scraping furiously over rough bark and I could imagine its flicking tail and swivelling head as it paused, midway up a tree, between darting runs.

At five fifty-five I braced myself and made the effort to drag my backside out of bed. I emerged from the tent into light drizzle. I clapped once and then explosively broke wind in order to scare away any bears.

"Bloody hell. Is it thundering?" came Gary's voice from inside the tent.

I followed up with an extravagantly loud burp and sauntered off to scent mark a tree. In the absence of the rest of civilization I was happily and rapidly regressing into a caveman state, unfettered by social niceties. After a luxurious pee I wandered over to last night's campfire where we had left the bear-proof barrels full of our clothes and food. I tried to thread my way through the berry bushes without letting them touch my long johns, not wanting to experience the discomfort that would follow their damp embrace. The trees did their benevolent best to shield me from the rain as I got dressed thirty metres or so from the tent. My fleece smelled faintly of smoke, an odour I already found vaguely comforting, conjuring up as it did, images of a warm campfire.

Gary was quick to follow my lead from the tent. He emerged carrying a haversack full of camera gear, probably hoping for the remains of a photogenic pink sunrise. Gary had spent the last fifteen years as a project engineer. It was a career he had fallen into rather than planned. At school he was good at maths and physics and so he had taken those subjects at 'A' level and then gone on to Brunel University to study engineering. His course had involved a year out in industry and during that year he had worked at British Steel on Teesside. On completion of his degree British Steel had offered him a job and he had taken it. He had become an engineer by fait accompli.

Photography has long been one of Gary's interests and this year, about three months before we had left for the Yukon he gave up his job to become a professional photographer. So both of us share an eye for the beauty of the natural world.

Breakfast was a tracker bar sloshed down with a cup of tea. As Gary drank his tea, sat on his life jacket and propped against a tree stump, he flipped through the pages of our guidebook, looking at the maps and trying to pick out obvious landmarks by which we could estimate our position. Gary is the planner, the navigator and generally, the brains of the operation. He also books the flights, the canoe rentals, sources maps and the like via the internet. I meanwhile, trail along in a vacuous capacity powering the canoe.

With the tea drunk and the cups rinsed and stowed away we began loading the gear into the canoe. The river was like glass, perfectly reflecting the mass of grey cloud overhead and the fringing riparian pines. A belted kingfisher rushed over the water, its twin keeping pace on the meniscus below. It stopped suddenly in mid-air, held aloft by blurring wings. Its head hung low, black dagger of a beak pointing to a target invisible to me. The wings folded and a tiny feathered missile lanced into the Teslin. It re-emerged, exploding upward through the ripples of its entry, a small fish struggling in its beak. Fish for breakfast.

We finished packing the gear into the canoe and pushed off into the river. The waterway was wide and the current sluggish. A harrier quartered the marshes on slender wings tipped with primary feathers that seemed to wave at us. It stooped and was gone. In the distance the humped blue-grey tops of hills poked out through a low bank of white cloud. Against the cloud the deep green of the pines stood out dramatically.

We quickly settled into the rhythm of the river. The paddle entered the water with a gentle 'plunk' and was followed by a gentle 'Schhh' as the fabric of my coat moved against itself during the stroke. As I completed the stroke a stream of droplets gently pattered over the river as the blade went forward to begin the cycle again. Otherwise the world was still. It felt good to be totally in control of my life. For the duration of this trip we would dictate our own schedule. We would camp when opportunity arose, get up when we felt like it, eat when we felt like it and rest when we felt like it. There would be no phone calls and no other demands on our time. Of course the weather might have a say in things and we were prepared to make alterations due to the dictats of bears and moose, but I didn't begrudge such instances.

The morning slid quietly by. At eleven-thirty the marshy bank on the right hand side of the river gave way to a wide gravel beach. With a cry of 'Hello Bear' we pulled over for lunch. With the canoe safely beached we busied ourselves making cheese sandwiches. Actually finding the stuff we needed such as plates, knives, margarine etc. would prove a slight kerfuffle every mealtime. We had two barrels crammed with stuff. One had, in the main, sleeping bags and clothes, whilst the other had the food. Everything was packed into separate carrier bags so that things were kept fresh or wouldn't melt, spill or contaminate each other and so that everything wasn't packed into one huge, unmanageable bag. After this meal the things we would need for the next would be below what we repacked now. There would then be exasperated searches for the one vital item that had sifted its way to the bottom of the barrel (the barrels had to be tipped in order to go back in the canoe, further enhancing the chaos inside).

As we ate, sat on our life jackets, I felt the chill in the air. As if the temperature wasn't reminder enough of the changing season, an aspen fluttered loudly behind us with uncountable jaundiced leaves.

Autumn is my favourite time of year. At these latitudes it is a season that lasts barely a fortnight, but at home it's a gentler affair lasting from early October to mid November. This year would be a bonus, as on my return from an autumn on the Teslin I would be in time to see the autumn on my home river, the Tees.

I remember walking down onto the riverbank of the Tees early one morning in late October. I was in woodland within Preston Park, three miles downstream of the market town of Yarm. There was a hard frost, which glittered blue and white in the bright sunshine. The grass felt brittle beneath my feet and as I entered the woods fallen leaves crunched in protest at my passing.

As I reached the riverbank I passed beneath a huge horse chestnut and at that moment a gust of wind caused a flurry of leaves to cascade down in a brown and gold blizzard. A flock of blue tits whirred amongst the undergrowth, ticking shrill calls as they went about their business. I sat on a log and watched the river before me, which was re-gathering its reflective mood now that the wind had subsided. The log had been there some years and had shed its bark revealing a hard surface dotted with the tiny holes made by some wood boring insects. There were thousands of holes but I couldn't recall ever seeing the creatures that had made them. The variety and fecundity of the invertebrate world is a constant source of amazement to me, yet so much of it is hidden and unknown.

A gentle plume of steam began to rise from the wooden fence in front of me as the frost sheathing it began to boil off in the strengthening sun. The light caught a dangling bunch of elder berries making their purple/black skin shine. A moorhen croaked and in the distance crows were quarrelling over something hugely important.

I stood up again and walked further along the river passing a spider's web finely bejewelled in water droplets. A jackdaw flew overhead with a single loud 'chack' and was lost amongst the browning crown of a beech. Suddenly there was a noise in the distance. At first it sounded like dogs but then I realized it was a flock of Canada geese. They flew towards me, honking and clamouring with a captivating exuberance. They circled overhead in a huge undulating skein, over a hundred strong in a riotous cacophony of life. They dipped towards the water and wings went back and legs came forward in unison. Air braking hard they hit the water to ski briefly and noisily over the Tees. With the sun behind them they were magnificent. It was a perfect autumn day.

The cheese sandwiches hit the spot. Though it might have been nice to digest for a few minutes, in the short time we had been ashore the cold had eaten into my thighs, which had started to ache, and it had insidiously worked its way under my coat. Needing to get moving in order to warm up we hurriedly reloaded the canoe and gladly resumed paddling.

The river remained stubbornly sluggish, its flow at its lowest ebb as the glaciers and snows of the mountains which fed it were re-freezing with the autumnal drop in temperature. The low water exposed mud in many places along the shore. Shades of rust, brown and purple coated the silt in a mosaic of algae. Slightly higher above the waterline the mud was hidden beneath a matt of bright green grass which moved in shimmering waves in the breeze. The movement of the grass was exaggerated by racing shadows as the clouds scudded under the sun. Much of the cloud was very low, white and filamentous and was an ineffective screen for the hills in the distance, which muscled through the gauze and appeared blue in the haze.

I felt very small and insignificant in this landscape, which indeed I was. The Yukon Territory is located in the far Northwest of

Canada. It is shaped like a wedge with the wide flat bottom against British Columbia, a straight edge running up along Alaska's border and the slope of the wedge running in from the Northwest Territory, coming to a point on the Arctic Ocean. The Southwest corner has the St Elias Mountains with Mount Logan at 5,950metres and the world's largest non-polar icecap. Heading north are the Ogilvie and Richardson Mountain ranges and much of the land, barring the mountain peaks and the northern tundra of the Arctic, is clothed in thick forest.

The Territory covers 483,450 square kilometres (208,000square miles), twice the size of Great Britain, but whilst Britain has a population of 60million, Yukon Territory has a population of 29,000. If the population were spread evenly over the Territory then each resident would have 20square kilometres to his or herself; but of course they aren't. Seventy-five percent of them live in Whitehorse and most of the rest inhabit Dawson and Watson Lake. Most of the Territory is uninhabited and for once, paddling in our tiny canoe, a throwback to prehistory, Gary and I were members of a rare species. It was an amazing feeling to look into the surrounding hills and know that nobody was there, hiking unseen amongst the timber. I thought that perhaps the giddyingly vast space around me was comparable to being a hiker in the centre of the English Lake District only there was nobody else within the National Park.

Towards the end of the afternoon the river narrowed dramatically and a steep hill rose up on the right bank. It was capped with a dense forest of pine, but the face of it was sparsely vegetated and there was much bare earth visible where landslides had scoured away the trees. To the left was a large bed of gravel and our tired arms pulled us, unconsciously at first, towards it. As the prow of the boat gently crunched ashore I hopped out and pulled the canoe parallel to the beach so that Gary could step out. My backside was grateful for the break as the seat of the canoe, though moulded, was hard plastic and my knees were similarly glad to assume a new position.

The central area of the gravel bank looked as if it had been there for some time, blushed as it was with green lichen and beyond its highest point a stream cut a silvered ribbon. Beyond the stream a semi-circular bay was bisected with a fallen pine which was still attached to the shore by a high root plate. Gary quickly scouted amongst the trees and came back, thumbs up. We unloaded the gear onto the high point of the berm and then carried the canoe to the tree line where we turned it over to protect it from overnight rain and then tied it to a tree in case of the unlikely event of a flash flood.

Amongst the trees was a perfect ready-made campsite. A circle of stones marked a campfire site and close by was a flat area underneath the pines where the tent could go. There were even logs cut and stood on end to serve as stools. As I came back down onto the gravel to get the last of my things I saw Gary stood stock still intently staring at something. He motioned me over with a tilt of his head and I slowly walked across the pebbles trying not to make too much noise.

"What is it?" I whispered.

"There's two muskrats amongst the branches of the fallen tree, about two thirds down."

I stared into the fallen tree, which for much of its length hovered within a foot of the river. It took a long moment before I could see them. They were huddled together, their coats a similar brown to the timber, in what looked like a nest amongst a tight group of branches. It was only a movement that helped my eyes to find them and when I did spot them, I was sure that I was seeing some weird creature with two tails until they shifted again and the two animals became clear. Muskrats are actually big voles, scaled up aquatic versions of a British bank vole. Instead of weighing 12-25gms they can weigh as much as a hefty 2kg.

Now that I had my eye in I could make out their blunt faces. One of them sat back on his, or her, haunches and it crouched like a little hairy ball. It's back feet sticking out in front of it were unfeasibly large, tipped with creamy coloured claws. As I watched it it picked up a twig and began to gnaw on it, shifting its weight and causing its tail to flop off the tree and dangle into the water. At this range I couldn't quite see it, but I knew that their tails are flattened at the sides to act as a rudder when swimming, which they do powerfully with slightly webbed rear feet. Its friend or mate plopped into the water and was gone. It could be as long as twenty minutes before it resurfaced.

The remaining muskrat settled down and curled up and with no action to watch we collected the rest of our stuff and got on with setting up the tent and getting firewood collected. Before embarking on the task of actually lighting the fire and cooking our meal we wandered back out onto the gravel bar to watch the sunset. From the crest of the beach we could look back along the river to the way we had come earlier. The cloud had lifted and broken up revealing patches of china blue. The clouds themselves were varying shades of grey and white and as the sun sank out of sight their undersides glowed pink. The mirror of the river reflected them perfectly, bordered on either side by the shaggy riverbanks. In the distance one small patch of forest was aglow with a golden light that had sneaked its way between the hills. Gary went calmly wild with his camera.

When the sun's fiery demise was complete we set about making our evening meal. Tonight would be chilli and mash, preceded by the usual barrel rummage. The purchase of food in Whitehorse had not gone entirely to my liking. When we had picked up our canoe from the rental company, Kanoe People, we had been expecting a lift to Johnson's Crossing. It turned out that something somewhere had been lost in the long distance communication and that the anticipated lift wasn't going to happen. However, Joanne McDougall, manager at Kanoe People, happily rang up her business rivals at 'Up North Adventures' on Strickland Street and they gamely came to our rescue. Kalin, the manager of Up North Adventures, was having two of his clients dropped off along the Canol road to descend the Nisutlin River and Johnson's Crossing was en route and there was room in the truck for us and our gear. But, instead of going later in the day as we had planned, they were due to leave within the hour.

We hadn't bought our food supplies yet and so the driver, Horst, dropped us at the supermarket on his way to pick someone up from a hotel. We had less than half an hour to get food for eight days with some spare emergency stuff. It was a supermarket sweep, both of us running up and down isles like neurotic ostriches. We sussed out ten evening meals, cheese for lunches with bread for the early days and crackers for further down-river and cereal bars for breakfasts. We also bought a lot of chocolate. Added to the tea bags, powdered milk and powdered mash we'd brought from Blighty we were sorted. Or so we sincerely hoped. There would be no popping out to the shop if we'd forgotten stuff. This is not the way I like to plan for my survival, but I had to live with it.

Back on the veranda of 'Up North', we packed the food into the bear barrels under the amused looks of Kalin and Horst. They seemed to find it hard to believe that not only had we done the shopping in the time allowed, but that we were going to survive on the stuff that we had bought, which admittedly looked like a lot of pasta and nothing fresh. I doubted we'd be away long enough to develop scurvy.

I squatted by the fire holding a long branch from which dangled a pot of water. I held it in the fire to get it boiling for the mash. There is nothing like cooking on a campfire. The flames keep you warm, cook your food and provide entertainment, after all who can resist staring into the flickering gyrations of combustion? As I prepped the mash, Gary heated the chilli and the two were brought to a sumptuous fusion. I have subsequently tried that particular brand of mash at home and it can only be described as nasty, but out in the woods it was the food of the gods.

It was my turn to relax whilst Gary did the washing up. I sat on my log stool, elbows on knees, and stared into the fire. How fantastic it felt to be finally here. The idea of canoeing on rivers in the Yukon Territory had been born in 1995. A series of hiking trips had led us to the Canadian Rockies where we were walking the 102-mile 'Caribou' section of the Great Divide Trail. One night we were camped in the woods, relaxing by our campfire and though the pines crowded thickly around us keeping us in gloom and holding our wood smoke captive amongst their branches, from somewhere a shaft of the dying sun warmed our backs and played in the blue air.

As we sat in silence a German guy appeared on the trail and asked to share our fire. Of course we assented and as he ate his evening meal we swapped stories of our travels. It transpired that he was in the German army and after a posting he could take several weeks off at a time. He told us that he had already been canoeing on the Yukon River and that as he had paddled along a bear had been swimming in the river and he had paddled alongside it! Now that sounded like adventure. That was for us. Two years later we were listening to wolves on the shores of Lake Laberge.

Our return to the Yukon and the Teslin River would be delayed by journeys in Kenya and Australia and by a kayaking trip in Glacier Bay, Alaska. There was also the small matter of me getting married in St Lucia. But those, as they say, are other stories. I now revelled in my return to the forest of the Yukon. Although Gary and I have been on many adventures we are just ordinary blokes, leading ordinary lives. Although working as a countryside ranger might sound different, glamorous even, I still work for the local council. My work is divided between managing nature reserves and other such areas, educational work with school children and events and guided walks for the public. I also do some talks and presentations for groups such as the Women's Institute, Rotary Clubs etc. Gary's job as a photographer sounds even more glam, but he spends much of his time locked away with his computer cleaning, filing and storing the images he has taken. Neither of us has any particular skill at canoeing, in fact we first went to the Yukon having never paddled a Canadian canoe before. We learnt as we went along. I'd like to say that we are two fit young men for whom such adventure should be a mere trifle, but at thirty-nine and forty years old, by anyone's standards we are middle aged; still fit though.

At some time in the early hours of the morning I woke up. I could feel an insistent pressure on my bladder and in days gone by I might have resisted it, hoping to fall back to sleep, but I knew it would be easier and I would be asleep quicker if I just got up and had a pee. I struggled upwards from my mummy sleeping bag and stuck my feet out of the tent and into my boots. Outside the stillness was incredible. There must have been a moon, because although I couldn't see it through the trees, there was light enough to see by. The silhouettes of the pines towering above me were living skyscrapers that stood totally motionless under a deep, deep blue sky. A thousand diamonds were scattered across the heavens and the air was crystalline and bitingly cold. My breath billowed, a silver cloud. Amongst the pines under such a sky I was truly awed. It would have been worth coming half way around the world just for that moment. I emptied my bladder and just as I was walking back to the tent there was a splash from the river. Instantaneously on one level I knew it was a leaping salmon, but on another my neurones shouted 'bear'. I jogged back into the tent with adrenaline fizzing through my veins.

Chapter Three

We were up at 6am. Last night's clear sky had been replaced with a thick fog. It slowly and steadily flounced around amongst the trees making sure that everything was damp. The air tasted of pine needles and soil and as I left the tent I felt a part of the earth. While Gary was cramming his sleeping bag into its stuff sac I ambled over to the fire. I made an executive decision to re-light it for breakfast whilst we waited for the fog to burn off, if indeed it was going to. I pushed the charred remains of last night's conflagration to the edge of the stone circle and filled the middle with some of the twigs and branches we had collected yesterday, but hadn't used.

As I knelt on one of the stones and its chill crept into the tendon below my knee, I thought I vaguely remembered reading somewhere that you shouldn't use rocks from a river to surround your fire as they had a tendency to explode. I briefly pondered the origin of these stones. Some of them did look rather smooth as if water worn. *'Bugger it,'* I thought *'they hadn't blown up last night'.* Using part of a paper shopping bag and some cardboard from a box of cereal bars as kindling, I coaxed a small flame into burning the damp twigs. After about ten minutes I had a decent fire going and I set about making up a breakfast of 'Hearty Soup' and tea.

As we drank our tea sat on the sawn-log stools by the fire the sun finally emerged as a pale white disc from behind the hill on the opposite side of the river. It forced its way through the pines, which it cast into jagged silhouettes partially obscured by tendrils of fog. It was an ethereal scene. Gary hadn't noticed the sun's appearance as he was facing the wrong way.

"Seen that," I nodded with my head.

"Oh, yeah," Gary replied.

He reached into the bag next to him and pulled out his camera. He stood up to get a shot but wanted more elevation to get above the trees growing on our side of the river. He put a foot on the log stool and sprang up. As his leg straightened the log flipped out from beneath him and he crashed down horizontally, the small of his back landing on the prone log. I was horrified, certain that he had broken his back.

"Are you okay?" I asked.

"I think so."

He rolled off the log and picked himself up. I felt a huge surge of relief. This was not the place to have a massive spinal injury. I had no doubt we could get word to the outside world that we were in trouble as there would be other canoeists coming past, but whoever did come by would take days to reach any civilization. Mobile phones were redundant here and not many people, including us, have satellite phones.

Gary picked up his camera and checked the display.

"Shit. There's an error message. I think I've broken my camera," he said.

Although I was extremely relieved that Gary was okay I couldn't help but being pissed off at him and I was annoyed with myself because the reason I was pissed off was totally selfish. On our return from our last wilderness trip, to Glacier Bay, Alaska, I had written a 2000-word article, which together with Gary's photos had been published in a national travel magazine called 'Global'. I intended to write another article about this trip, but without photographs there would be little hope of getting it published. It was my aim to use my articles as a way of being recognized as a writer and thus as a springboard to getting a novel written and published. My dreams of authorship receded into the distance, hand in hand with my dreams of a winning lottery ticket.

"The casing's cracked," Gary announced.

He tried to take the lens off but it was stuck fast. After some furious wrestling it finally came away revealing that the mount was bent out of alignment. We didn't have any tools with us so Gary set about the task of trying to square things back up again with the tip of my penknife blade. Unable to offer any help and resigned to a writing career stifled at birth, I sat back down to finish my tea.

I watched as the sun continued it's inexorable ascension into the sky. My eyes were then drawn down to my cup of tea by the movement of the steam rising from it. In the growing light I thought I could see individual droplets of vapour swirling into the air, jostling with their neighbours in the breeze of convection.

"I think it's usable," Gary said, breaking into my reverie. "There doesn't seem to be light getting in and the picture looks okay, except it may be slightly blurred along the right hand edge. Look."

He handed the camera over and I looked at the picture of the trees he had just taken. I wasn't sure if I could see blurring or not and I said so.

"I'll just have to hope for the best and check it out on a computer in Carmacks or Dawson," he said as I handed the camera back.

Gary bunched his left fist and then opened it out, stretching his fingers. He grimaced with pain.

"You okay?" I asked.

"I've hurt my arm. I didn't notice at first. I think I was too shocked by the fall and concerned about the camera, but it's really hurting now."

"How bad?"

"Really bad."

"What? Broken bad?"

"Yeah, I think so. It feels like it did in Argentina."

Three years ago Gary had broken the same elbow hiking up a snow clad mountain in Argentina on an overland expedition. It had been a week before his party had reached a town, by then in Chile, with a hospital and the break was diagnosed and set in plaster.

"Oh you plank. What the hell did you stand on a wobbly log for?" I railed.

"I know, I know."

"I promised Mel we wouldn't do owt stupid. She is never going to let me out of the house again."

My wife, Melanie, had not wanted me to come on a wilderness trip. 'What happens if you have an accident?' she had asked.

'We won't. I'll be dead careful. Hikers don't jump' I had replied.

'What do you mean?' She had asked.

'I mean if a careful hiker comes across an obstruction, like a fallen tree, he climbs up it and climbs back down. He doesn't jump down, because he could twist an ankle or worse. I'll do everything to minimize risk and if one of us does have an accident the other one will just paddle him out. I'm a first aid instructor. We'll be alright.'

"Maybe you've just banged a nerve," I said, mentally clutching at straws.

There was no swelling, no disfigurement and there was still movement, so it wasn't beyond the realms of possibility.

"Yeah, it's possible. I'll see how it goes this morning."

I fervently hoped it went okay during the morning because otherwise instead of enjoying a holiday we could be facing the very survival situation Mel had feared. I thought grimly that the Teslin may just have metamorphosed into that well-known waterway, 'Shit Creek'. At least we still had both paddles.

"Let's get the gear loaded," I said.

The sun was by now in the ascendancy and a perfect day was beginning. We hauled the gear down onto the shore, Gary with one arm, in preparation for loading. Before we did load the boat we went back into the woods to search for sticks. They needed to be three to four feet long and have a decent girth. They would become an essential part of our equipment to be stowed away with the boat and reused each day. Laid in the bottom of the canoe in a criss-cross pattern we put our rucksacks on them. This kept our bags above the bottom of the concave hull and so if it rained any water that came on board would slosh around below our stuff.

The barrels were laid down in front of the bags behind the front seat and the tent was packed down the side. All the gear was then tied together and lashed to a seat with a thin mountaineering rope. If we capsized at least all our stuff would stay together, although thoughts of capsizing didn't bear thinking about. Laid over all the equipment and similarly tied in, we placed the tarp. This was a sheet of plastic roughly six feet by six feet that had metal eyeholes along its edges. This was used in the boat to keep rain and splashes off everything else and when we camped we could lash it up as a shelter to cook under in case of rain.

Finally on the water the river had narrowed considerably and the marshes fringing the banks were lost and replaced by cliffs and forest. I sat in the front of the boat with Gary behind, where if his arm became too painful to paddle he would at least be able to steer. The sunshine was glorious and the sky an azure blue. I remembered being at primary school and asking a teacher why the sky was blue. He looked flummoxed for a moment and then told me it was a reflection of the sea. Years later I remembered that when I found out that the sky is blue because of the water vapour in the air. As sunlight passes through the air each droplet acts as a prism scattering the light. The wavelength of light that's scattered the most is blue. So we have blue sky by a quirk of physics.

The current had picked up to push us along. A raven whirled in the air close to us revealing the iridescent gloss of its feathers. I love ravens. Their calls vary from deep crow-like 'kronks' and 'kaws' to burbles and whistles. Drawn on by the river with ravens for company I was exhilarated.

For the native peoples of the Northwest coast the raven has a special significance. According to the Tlingit people the early world was populated with Original People who had human characteristics, but not always human form. There were people like Sun, Moon, Raven and Eagle. In the earliest days the world was a place of darkness because the sun was kept in a box by the Sky Chief. Raven had become bored flying around in the dark and so he made a hole in the clouds to gain access to the sky-world. Once there he changed into a pine needle floating in a cup of water. Sky-Chief's daughter took a drink from the cup and swallowed the needle, which made her pregnant.

Presently Sky-Chief's daughter gave birth to a baby boy who was really raven in disguise. The child constantly asked to play with the box containing the sun and like all indulgent grandfathers, Sky-Chief eventually relented. At that point Raven changed back into his bird-form and flew back to earth with the box. On his return Raven was hungry and he came upon some fishermen whom he asked for some food. They refused and so raven flew on. Eventually, he met an old chief who did give him something to eat. Raven took out the box for the old chief and opened it up. The world became a place of light and the fishermen who had refused Raven food were turned into frogs.

In Tlingit folklore Raven is portrayed as a trickster and a shape changer and someone whose curiosity gets him into trouble. It was Raven who gave the world fresh water, which again, he had stolen. It had been the sea bird, Petrel, who had made a house over the only freshwater spring in the world. Raven wanted water so that people could drink and so the fish would have somewhere to swim to. Before he set off to steal the water he preened his feathers which at the time were white.

Petrel wouldn't let Raven anywhere near the spring, despite Ravens best attempts to lure him away. Eventually, when Petrel fell asleep Raven covered him in mud and then shouted to wake him. Petrel, realizing he was filthy, rushed away to get clean and Raven began drinking the fresh water. As Petrel returned Raven dashed for the smoke hole in the roof to make his escape, but Petrel called to the smoke hole spirits,

"Grab him, hold him."

Raven was temporarily trapped but managed to wriggle free, though his feathers were coated in soot. As he flew away he tried to preen himself and as he did so droplets of water fell from his beak to form the earth's glaciers, lakes and rivers. From that day forward Raven's feathers remained jet black.

It was also thanks to Raven that the rivers are full of fish. He had tricked Seagull into giving him some eulachon (a small fish from which the Tlingit people obtain fish oil). Raven then set about boasting how he had caught them in a river. The chief who owned all the fish was very angry at hearing this boast and he rushed back to his house to check the fish trap beneath it. He was in such hurry that he accidentally let the fish out, thus stocking the rivers and seas with fish.

Up ahead on the river was an island that, Gary told me, our guidebook advised us to keep to the left of, as the right side was perilously shallow. As we approached, the scent of pine filled my nostrils making me feel a part of the forest, which cradled the river. It was a subtle smell, not at all like the contrived pine scent added to toilet cleaners and air fresheners. We whipped around a bend in the river to the left of the island, speeding up in the current, which was now funneled into a tighter space. Suddenly, we were in shade and there, protected from the sun, a low mist lingered in a filamentous platinum swirl. I was so entranced by the experience I had to hold in the urge to shout for joy, for it would have been unseemly to shatter the peace. All thoughts of Gary's accident were driven from my head.

In moments the island was left behind and we rejoined the sun on a shining river of silver. Up front in the canoe I was keeping my eyes peeled for wildlife, but I had to keep an eye out for the river as well. There were many places where it burbled over riffled sections only inches deep. I had to find the deeper channels, usually on the outside of bends and call out to Gary which way to steer. The frequent gravelly islands were tricky, as often it was difficult to tell which side to go until it was very late. Sometimes the decision was made easier because the volume of water going one way would pull the boat into the deeper water, but sometimes there was no such clue and we ended up making last minute changes and having to paddle like hell to avoid the shallows.

Huge salmon in bright red livery occasionally jumped clear of the water and their carcasses littered some of the beaches. These were Chinook, or King, salmon, which can reach 120cm in length and weigh 40lbs. Between May and July they had been spawning, but now that their frenzied breeding was over they were dying. A bald eagle, the first of many such perambulators, strode about amongst the pebbles looking for fish. As we approached he took to the air and was momentarily suspended in a head wind. His feet dangled, immense talons pointing downward from loose toes, his legs clothed in brown baggy trousers of feathers. His wings beat the air and he was propelled gracefully away, low over the water, wingtips skimming the surface carefree millimetres from disaster.

Ravens too haunted the beaches looking for fish carcasses. Sometimes they stood or perched in pairs like hunched old men, suspiciously watching our passage. In a particularly narrow section of the river a beaver swam upstream close to our boat with nose pointing skyward and nostrils flared. Its tail splashed the water behind it as if it were being chased by a small breadboard.

A flock of six mergansers played chase with us. As we drew level with them they raced off downstream, skittering over the surface paralleling the bank. They are attractive birds with powdery grey sides, a white collar and brown heads. They dive for a living, going after fish with their long serrated beak. After two races, five of them took off leaving one to compete with the boat twice more before it too took off to go and do something less trivial. They were a delight to watch.

The river opened out and we were confronted with a maze of gravel bars. In every direction there was shallow water bubbling over the substrate and no obvious main route. I gambled on a route and lost. We bumped and scraped and pushed for perhaps twenty feet into our chosen riffle when we ground to a halt.

"Shite!" I cursed. "After three…"

This was a manoeuvre we had learned before on the Yukon.

"One, two three."

At that point we pushed our paddles back against the riverbed whilst lifting bums off seats and pushing the canoe forward with our feet. We crunched a little bit further, onto higher land.

"Bollocks," said Gary.

I looked behind me and Gary was already unlacing his boots.

"You takin' your boots off?" I asked surprised.

Strictly speaking this was a no-no. Scrambling about in cold water over slippery rocks in your bare feet is a recipe for disaster. On the other hand, I looked at the pebbles below me to see that they were smooth and seemingly free of jagged edges. I didn't relish putting my feet in the water as it looked as cold as it was clear, but I didn't fancy having wet boots for the next few hours either.

"Alright. Might as well. In for a penny, in for a pound," I muttered and took my boots off, consoling myself with the fact that the water was only inches deep.

It wasn't as if we were wading in deep water where we wouldn't be able to see where we placed our feet. We stood in water that was several degrees below bracing with our trousers rolled up like day-trippers to Blackpool. An eagle flew directly overhead screaming a note of ridicule at us. We gingerly shuffled the boat ten or fifteen feet further on into a pool of water at least two feet deep. From our perch at the end of the riffle we re-boarded. I sat with my feet drip-drying for a few minutes whilst we let the canoe drift in a lazy semi-circle. I had anticipated them feeling really cold, but now that they were out of the water even the cool air felt warm. After I dried the residual water off with a towel and put my socks back on my feet were in heaven. I silently thanked Gary for taking his boots off, for if he hadn't I wouldn't have and we would now be sitting in wet boots. Ray Mears, I'm sure, would have had a fit.

We passed numerous bald eagles perching in trees, on logs and walking around on gravel bars. In the late afternoon we went beneath a high clay cliff on the right hand side of the river and in the air above the cliff top were four eagles wheeling lazily on thermals. Two ravens came bolting from the trees to buzz them and I was put in mind of spitfires coming out to attack bigger bombers. Swiftly the attackers became the attacked, but the river was taking us out of view and so the outcome of the battle was unknown.

On our right Indian River joined the Teslin from behind a large mound of pebbles and rocks. We landed immediately after the confluence and scouted out the area for a campsite. It was 5pm and we were glad of the rest. Indian River was less than ten metres wide and it rushed quickly over its rocky bed, throwing up small patches of white water. Conscious that the sound of the racing river might mask the sound of our landing we clapped and shouted as we explored amongst the scrubby riverside willows and the pines behind them.

We found a well used area for a camp. Someone had kindly fashioned benches out of fallen logs right next to a campfire ringed with stones. When the tent was up and the canoe secured, we lit a fire to heat our meal and water for a cup of tea. The late sun was burnishing the trees and us with a golden light, further enhanced by the flames of the fire. If I stood absolutely still I could feel the warmth of the sun begin to heat my fleece, but if I moved, the swirl of the cold air around me stole the fledgling warmth. I sat down by the fire and let Indian River lull us with its constant melody from only twenty metres away.

"How's the arm?" I asked Gary as we waited for the water to boil.

"Sore. I gave up paddling mid-morning and was just steering. Did you notice?"

"No, you're a piss weak paddler anyway."

"Cheers. I hope it stops throbbing by tomorrow 'coz I couldn't even hold my camera to get photos by late morning."

He was holding his wrist in his left hand and cradling his forearm against his thigh taking the weight out of his elbow.

"Do you want me to make a sling?" I asked.

"Yeah. What with?"

"Have you got a fleecy top spare?"

"Yep," and with that he went to root through his clothes. When he came back I tied the arms behind Gary's neck and used the neck of the fleece to support his wrist.

"How's that?" I asked.

"Pretty good."

With Gary more comfortable in a sling I made our evening meal and reluctantly washed up afterwards in the ice cold water of Indian River. Later I moved away from the fire and stepped out from the trees onto the riverbank to watch the last of the sun settle behind the hills. The river was open territory and away from the embrace of the forest it felt like I had stepped outside. A breeze tugged at my clothes and the river seemed to exhale a frigid breath. The black spectre of a raven flew gracefully overhead, for once without uttering a cry.

When I returned to the fire Gary was poring over our river guide.

"I reckon we've done thirty-one miles today," he announced.

"How many miles do we need to do every day?" I asked.

Our mileage, now that Gary was incapacitated as a paddler, was something we would need to monitor. We had given ourselves a generous eight days to reach Carmacks, but we couldn't afford to be late. Buses to Dawson from Carmacks didn't run every day and we didn't want to waste vital days kicking our heels- we wanted time to explore Dawson and to drive the Dempster Highway.

"We need to aim at thirty miles a day."

I let that sink into my brain. We had done that today, just. But we had paddled until five in the afternoon. We may have lost the luxury of stopping at three and goofing around. Our progress could slow by a considerable amount if we hit long stretches of still water combined with a headwind. Thankfully we had canoed on the Yukon before and we knew that its current was considerably swifter than the Teslin's had been so far. Although the Yukon leg would be half the journey in mileage, it would hopefully be less time-wise.

Chapter Four

I awoke at six to the sound of rushing water. Close by, Indian River was racing enthusiastically to its meeting with the Teslin, but Indian River was only making a part of the roar I was hearing. My mind was adding to the watery serenade of the real rivers by conjuring up something much wilder. As my consciousness swam up from the depths of my slumber the roaring subsided to be replaced by a twinge in my stomach. I knew the source of my anxiety as I remembered that today would be the day we would tackle 'Roaring Bull Rapids.'

I urged myself to chill out a bit. There would be nothing to worry about. Our river guide assured the reader that the rapids were more of a ride to enjoy than a hazard, but still, thoughts of capsizing kept racing unwanted and incessantly into my head like a horsefly at a picnic. Perhaps the rapids might be okay under normal circumstances, but what if we needed to make some sharp corrections to our course, or needed a burst of speed? Such manoeuvres would be limited by Gary's arm. 'Calm down Bob, don't be a fanny,' I scolded myself.

I got dressed in another morning fog. Gary got up as I left the tent and we telepathically agreed to get a fire going. I looked for some wood whilst Gary rummaged in the food barrel for a packet of soup. The fire and the soup helped to take my mind off the rapids.

"I don't suppose you can wash up with a busted arm," I said to Gary.

He smiled and shook his head.

"You better not be jerking my chain so I'll do all the washing up," I said as I gathered up the pots and made my way down to Indian River. The soup had been spot welded to the bottom and sides of the pan and the pain of trying to remove it in the icy water with a pan scourer but no soap, completely cleared my head of thoughts of Roaring Bull Rapids. I sat back to warm my hands and watched the fog swirl around the treetops in an ethereal embrace.

Before I let my hands get too comfortable there was one more job to do-filter some water. We were to get all our drinking water from the streams entering the river and though it looked sparklingly pure, and probably was, there was a risk that it may carry a protozoan known as *Giardia lamblia.* Drinking infected water could result in sickness and diarrhoea. As giardia is well known to be carried in beaver faeces, the symptoms resulting from an infection are often known as beaver fever; honestly.

I don't like adding chemicals such as iodine to my drinking water and boiling it is time consuming and uses a lot of fuel, so Gary and I have a mechanical filter, roughly the size of two clenched fists and which works via a hand pump. Pumping the filter is a bit of a chore, but it only takes ten minutes to fill the bladder and our water bottles. We tend to use the tributary streams and rivers as a source of water as they have less silt in them than the main river and so are less likely to block the filtration system. I pumped away.

As I finished collecting the water and stood up I noticed the exuvia, (the empty nymphal skin), of a dragonfly under a lip of one of the boulders by the rivers edge. I love to investigate tiny creatures such as these, as the minutiae of life fascinates me. I find life on earth wondrous. The profusion and diversity of it is staggering and yet the species we see today are only around 1% of the total number of species that there has ever been. Life is made all the more colossally stupendous by the fact that it has arisen, through a process of natural selection, from single celled creatures in response to environmental change. Hardly a day goes by when I don't contemplate how special life is.

I marvelled at the delicate beauty of the empty skin, appreciating the miracle of it and the fact that it was still here despite the wind and rain. The nymphs of dragonflies live in water where, considering they are predators, they lead a remarkably sedentary life. Like their parents, they have six legs with which they can move and stalk prey, but for the most part they just wait in ambush.

They can tackle prey as large as fish fry with a remarkable set of mandibles. Their lower 'lip' is hugely enlarged and tipped with a fearsome pair of hooks. The whole assemblage is folded up underneath the head and as in this position it conceals much of the animal's head, it is known as the 'mask'. When a victim is spotted the mask shoots out under hydrostatic pressure as far as a centimetre, lancing the prey with the hooks and drawing it back to the mouth to be consumed.

The nymphs breathe in an unusual way. Their rectum is highly convoluted forming a surface over which gas exchange can take place. Water is sucked in and subsequently expelled and this expulsion can be done with quite some force enabling the animal to propel itself with a squirt of water.

As the nymph ages it grows via a series of moults, each post-moult nymph being known as an instar, until it is ready to metamorphose into the adult form. Prior to metamorphosis the young of many insects, known as larvae, change into a pupa and their subsequent metamorphosis is said to be complete. However, in some insects, rather than forming a pupa, the skin of the final instar splits open and the adult emerges. This is incomplete metamorphosis and the young of such insects are known as nymphs. The term incomplete metamorphosis seems ridiculous in the face of the change seen as the winged and bejewelled adult emerges from the drab skin of the final instar.

I left the husk of the long departed dragonfly and went to get my camera to take some photos of the fog, the trees and the river. Gary was already composing atmospheric masterpieces with his camera and after a few more minutes we were ready to load up and go.

With the input of the Indian and Boswell rivers behind us we seemed to be pushed on a little faster at first and I didn't have long to fret over the approach of Roaring Bull Rapids as they were soon upon us. The fog had receded to a swirling mist as the river widened out into an inverted heart shape. A large island covered the left ventricle and gravel bars covered much of the right, with small channels either side. As the river closed again at the heart's apex, the water spilled out over the rapids beneath high clay cliffs.

As we closed in, the rapids appeared as a line of disturbed water, only occasionally breaking into white horses. We took a line close to the right-bank and did nothing more than steer as we careened through the rough water. It was over in a minute and the burst of speed had been a thrill, greatly enhanced by the relief of our survival. Roaring Bull my ass, it was more the Moo of a Cow.

As Mooing Cow Rapids receded behind us we were still enveloped in a damp, chilling mist and I was glad of the exertion of paddling to keep me warm. Gary didn't have that luxury. His arm was too painful to actively paddle and he was freezing. By putting the shaft of the paddle against the boat on the right-hand side he could pinch it there with his right hand. This was the broken arm, but sat as he was, the arm could rest in the sling whilst his hand gripped. With his left hand on the top of the paddle he could swing the blade in the water to steer. As he could only steer on this side of the boat it meant that I had to continually paddle with the same arm and I didn't have the luxury of swapping over. Still, I hardly had room to complain.

We settled into the peace of the morning. Gary and I canoe without talking. We share the experience with no need to break the spell of the wilderness. Our only communication is to point out danger, or the route, or something of exceptional beauty, usually an animal or bird, but sometimes just a mountain or a tree. We don't chatter.

This general lack of communication seems odd to some, especially my wife, Melanie, who is a great one for talking. She can speak to her friend Pauline for an hour on the phone even though they might have seen each other that day and may be seeing each other the next. Pauline's husband once threatened to put her in a taxi and send her round to our house because he reckoned it would be cheaper than the phone bill.

I remember sitting in the lounge on my return from our last Yukon trip. I was sat on the windowsill of the bay window and the September sunlight was streaming in warming my back and lighting Mel in a warm glow.

"How's Gary getting on with Anna?" she asked, referring to Gary's girlfriend at the time.

"Dunno," I replied.

"What, didn't you ask him?" she asked incredulously.

"No."

"Why not?"

"Dunno," I shrugged. "Never came up."

"What the hell did you two talk about for four weeks in the middle of nowhere?"

"Dunno. This and that, but the wildlife gets scared off by voices."

"Surely you talked at night though?"

I just looked out of the window and shrugged.

"You don't talk at all do you?" she said, exasperated, "You just grunt at each other."

Looking back at our trip on the Teslin I can see that perhaps it would have been good if we had spoken more to each other. I didn't know at the time that Gary was sat behind me cursing himself endlessly for jumping up onto the log and hurting his arm, which although he was confident hadn't put us in any real danger, it might possibly ruin our holiday. He felt extremely guilty that it was now down to me to paddle us out. I wish he had told me that, or that I had asked him, because I really didn't mind doing the paddling, even if at the time I thought, rather harshly, that he was a daft bugger.

The mist finally cleared by 10.30am revealing an overcast day. The low hills and the pines stood out in stark contrast against the pale washed out sky. Great lengths of the riverbanks were fringed by wide areas of gently sloping pebbles and we saw several bald eagles walking over the stones in search of stranded and dying salmon.

By the time we washed up on such a beach for our lunch the temperature had hardly risen since first light and when we got out of the canoe both of us were shivering as if we had ague. I ran up and down the shore a few times to try to warm up. 'Running' is probably a generous description of my actions, as a combination of canoeing cramp in my arse and legs and wobbly stones beneath my feet, made me stagger about like a drunken foal. I got breathless but not really any warmer. 'This will be okay,' I thought to myself as I ran around. We were making good progress even though I was the only one paddling. Gary seemed in less pain now with the sling taking some of the strain and he had recovered enough movement to handle his camera easily. We had survived the rapids and I was back to enjoying the trip as a holiday rather than worrying about a survival situation.

During the afternoon the river alternated between long narrow sections and then areas where it opened out and was littered with islands and gravel bars and throughout the afternoon numerous ravens and eagles monitored our progress. The forest around us was dense with pine but gaily splashed with the yellows and golds of the autumnal aspens, cottonwoods and birch.

Up ahead my eye was drawn towards a movement. Sat on a prominent boulder jutting into the river, was a mink. It stood tall in profile to us, studying something on the far shore. A golden leaf from an aspen behind it suddenly fluttered down and helicoptered close by its head en route to a splashdown in the river. The mink turned to watch its passage and then saw us. By now we were only about ten metres away. It was good to see a mink in its natural home. We have mink in Britain, but they are not the mink of continental Europe, but descendants of American mink that escaped or were released from fur farms. Its pelage was a beautiful chocolate brown with a small white beard and it looked at us with eyes of sparkling coal. With a mere five metres between us it leapt into the river and submerged. I felt a tiny thump beneath my feet as it rose back up against the hull of the canoe and then emerged on the far side only to dive once more and be lost.

By 3pm the river had widened yet again and become braided, forcing us to constantly choose routes through ominously shallow riffles.

"Hey Gaz," I called to Gary. "We'll pull over 'coz I could do with a dump."

"Right. Got a spot in mind?"

"How about there," I pointed with my paddle to a place where the bank dipped from a ten-foot high ridge right down to the waterline.

"Okey-dokey."

The bow of the canoe turned right with a hiss as Gary steered us in towards our landing. The prow crunched ashore, though the pebble bank wasn't large enough to get the boat fully beached. I leapt out with a 'hello bear', Gary behind me holding onto the bow rope.

I rummage in one of the barrels for the toilet paper and a lighter and I got the trowel from a pocket in my rucksack. Suitably equipped for the job I squeezed my way into the willow scrub. The soil was sandy and kicked up in front of my boots. I headed up a slope and found myself in a gully, which in all likelihood became a stream in wet weather. 'Bollocks,' I thought, 'I can't have a crap in here 'coz I'll pollute the watercourse.' Just as I thought that I almost stumbled over a huge bear scat. Incredibly there was a berry sat on top of it in almost pristine condition. Bears obviously don't give a shit about where they shit, considerations of watercourses be damned.

They are truly impressive animals and I've always been amazed at how big and powerful they are (a big brown bear can stand nine feet tall on its back legs and weigh 70 stone) given that the majority of their diet is made up of tiny berries. They are unfussy omnivores so as well as eating berries and nuts, they dig up tubers, chew buds and leaves, root out insects and catch fish, scavenge carcasses and kill animals such as deer, caribou and moose.

Despite eating a lot of plant material they aren't very good at digesting it as the berry triumphantly sat on top of this turd testified. Bears haven't the cellulose digesting gut fauna that ruminants like cows and sheep have. The root of the problem is that they are carnivores that have gone partially veggie out of the necessity to be able to eat anything they come across in order to maintain their bulk. The problem with being a carnivore is that you might not be able to catch anything to eat for long spells and being able to eat anything takes the sting out of a boom and bust diet. In our common parlance carnivore is now taken to mean 'meat eater' but that isn't an accurate definition. A dolphin catches and kills vertebrate prey (fish) and so could be called a meat eater, but it isn't a true carnivore. The term is a zoological order reserved for those animals that have evolved from an ancestral animal with specialized meat slicing molar teeth known as carnassials. Bears have carnassials and so do dogs, the mouths of which are a lot easier to peek inside for a look without getting killed. (Incidentally the teeth of the dolphin are all just simple sharp pegs).

Ursus arctos is the scientific name for the brown bear. It means bear bear, the 'ursus' is Latin and the 'arctos' is Greek. It's the quintessential bear. Brown bears used to roam all over North America as far south as Mexico and similarly they used to roam over Europe as far south as North Africa, but those days are long gone. Unlike the black bear, brown bears can roam up above the tree line and out onto the tundra. Without the escape route of trees they have got to be big enough to take care of themselves.

Brown bears need plenty of room in order to find enough food- a males' territory averages some 80-800 square miles. The real problem of eating a lot more fruit and other vegetation for northern bears is the food-free winter. The way around winter is to sleep through it. Some hibernating animals, such as bats, conserve their energy stores by shutting down their metabolic processes and reducing their body temperature to just above freezing. Several times during the winter they wake up to drink, perhaps eat some cached food and eliminate waste. Other slightly bigger animals such as racoons and skunks stay at near normal temperatures but also sleep, conserving energy by surviving on a thick layer of fat. Bears do a combination of both. Their temperature falls, but only by about four degrees Celsius, whilst their breathing and heart rate fall considerably. They too store up large amounts of fat to stay warm. They are the only mammals capable of going six months without food or drink and without urinating or defecating. If a human being were to lie in bed for six months his/her muscles would waste away, but a bear maintains its musculature by recycling products that would normally be lost in urine.

I took a good look at that pile of scat. It was comfortingly old, dried out by the wind and sun. I tried to imagine the bear that dropped it and wondered what it thought of this area as a place to live. Was it having a successful life as a bear, had it raised cubs, or was it a male, or was it too young for offspring? Female bears don't breed until they are five to ten years old and they wait two to five years before putting themselves through the ordeal of raising kids again. They will typically live for twenty-five years in the wild.

I clapped loudly again and climbed up out of the gully looking for a likely spot to complete my mission.

It was 3.30pm when we finally made landfall on a huge semi-permanent island of sand and gravel. From the waterline there was a gently shelving beach stretching over a hundred metres before there was any ground stable enough to support vegetation. The green oasis at the head of the beach was where we headed.

The centre of the island was covered in scrubby willow rooted in amongst sand trapped in the gravel. We pitched the tent on the biggest patch of contiguous sand we could find, an area roughly five metres by five metres. It was an ideal spot, perfectly flat and firm without any lumps. We weighted the guy lines down with rocks, as the sand wouldn't hold tent pegs. The air had the feel of rain to it so we rigged up the tarp as a shelter to sit beneath in case it arrived whilst we were preparing our meal. We attached guy lines from each corner of the tarp to deadfall trees and made an 'A-frame' roof by propping it up with the paddles.

We made our fire amongst the stones on a berm and fuelled it with driftwood of which there was plenty.

"We ain't gonna run out of firewood," I said to Gary as I threw down an armful by our fledgling fire. "There's a shit load of wood here."

"A shit-load? Is that a new S.I unit? How many shit-loads are there in a metric tonne?" Gary asked.

I cast my eye over the beach assessing the mass of timber. Whole trees had washed up here in huge logjams over twelve feet high which themselves, had acted as magnets for further floaters. The carcasses lay in silent testimony to the power of the river and to the fecundity of their species. The driftwood sticks I had gathered so far felt smooth to the touch, the rough bark having gone and the wood underneath almost polished. It felt unusually light as well, like balsa wood, the sun having driven out the heavy moisture and bleached its skeleton.

"I reckon looking at this lot, that there are about 10tonnes to a shit-load," I pontificated.

Gary nodded sagely and went off to gather some more wood.

As I zigzagged over the beach collecting branches that weren't too big (we hadn't brought an axe or saw to save on the amount of gear we would have to carry when we ditched the canoe in Carmacks) the afternoon became hazy. The mountains in the distance turned various shades of blue, fading to black and the sky above was so huge that when I looked up I had felt a slight sense of agoraphobia.

By the time we were eating our meal of chilli and mash the sun was in the final stages of its descent. The rain had held off and although there was virtually no wind the air was bitingly cold. We sat on our life jackets insulating our backsides from the chill of the sand, with our backs resting against a driftwood tree. In front of us the fire danced vigorously, an orange beacon in the gathering dusk. The trees on the far bank stood proud of the water above a river-cliff of clay. The white trunks of aspen shone like skinny ghosts amongst the pine, their canopies explosions of yellow. I watched carefully for any signs of movement, but there were none and it was rapidly becoming too dark to see that far.

I watched the flickering flames of the fire and thought about the day we had just enjoyed. I had been needlessly worried about the rapids, as they had turned out to be a thrill rather than a fearsome obstacle. But looking out over the river thinking about the nature of fear took me back to the one time in my life that I have been truly terrified.

In 1989 I spent nearly six months backpacking in the US. I had started my journey in Florida and had spent several weeks in a youth hostel in Fort Lauderdale. I had made a lot of friends amongst the travellers there and several of us met up again in New Orleans, where a group of us got an apartment on the edge of the Faubourg Marigny district of town, separated from the French Quarter only by the width of Esplanade Avenue.

As the days went by and more of the Florida crowd arrived, space in the flat became scarce and I offered to make room by sleeping in my Chevrolet van. It was a compact and bijou residence, kitted out as it was with a foam mattress. I had parked it across the street outside a bar called 'The Dream Palace'. The bar was a rustic kind of a place but it was our favourite haunt as it was very close and had a pool table and a good selection on the jukebox. Like many of the bars in 'The Big Easy' it was open twenty-four hours a day.

During the early hours of one morning I was awakened by the sound of shouting. I sat up and looked out through the windscreen of the van. It was beaded with condensation but with the aid of the streetlights I could see two men having an argument. One of them was black and the other white and they were at it hammer and tongs, some of the abuse they were dishing out was racial in nature. The shouting abruptly stopped when the fists started flying and then the white guy kicked the black guy in the head after he had doubled him over from a previous blow. With that the white guy stalked off and the loser picked himself up and staggered back into the bar.

It had all been over in less than a minute and I settled myself back to sleep. Some time later I was awakened again by more shouting and when I sat up the same white guy was stood right in front of the van. His arms were stretched out holding what I instinctively knew was a gun. It was that classic pose you see on the TV where the cop is holding his gun straight out with both hands shouting at the perp. to put down his gun. I saw the muzzle flash and heard the bang as one.

From across the street someone returned fire. That round smacked the windscreen with a glancing blow making an instant spider web with a six-inch diameter. As the back of the van had no windows and my view was restricted to the windscreen I could only assume, correctly as it turned out, that the other gunman was the black guy from the earlier fight.

I flung myself backward to lie flat on my back. I was acutely aware that the sides of the van were very thin metal and were unlikely to stop the passage of a bullet. I was terrified. I could feel adrenaline rush out of my adrenals in time with my heartbeat with the burning cold of liquid nitrogen.

The guy in front of the van fired again and then ran to my right as another shot replied from across the street. As the 'fight or flight' hormone poured into my bloodstream I couldn't do either and my muscles went into a spasm. I tried to lay flat to make myself less of a target, but my back arched upwards as my fingertips and heels pushed against the mattress. I have never been so terrified and felt so helpless and I sincerely hope that I never feel that terror again.

Outside the rounds were coming thick and fast. According to my friends, who watched the whole thing from the window of the flat, the black guy had run across the street and the pair of them were now running around the van shooting at each other, in a dreadful parody of two kids playing 'tig' around a tree.

I seemed to lie there for a glacial age, but in reality it only took seconds for both of them to run out of ammo and run off in different directions before the cops arrived. I lay there panting, wild eyed and twitching as the police did a quick look around the street, popped into the Dream Palace and then drove off.

I got up and went into the bar where Bob, the barman, took one look at my ashen face and asked,

"Were you out there in van?"

He had seen the gunfight through the bar window. I nodded and he poured me a big whiskey. As I downed that my friend Phil Decter, an amiable Bostonian, entered the bar to check on me. We went back up to the flat where I was fussed over and made to drink sweet tea, which made me feel sick. I was shaking like a leaf for at least half an hour and was so strung out on adrenaline that I could hardly sit.

Phil and I went back out onto the street where the dawn was just starting to blush the sky. We picked up three cartridge cases and a distorted bullet from the road, which I still have to this day and then we set out to walk off my fear.

As the sun sank, its final rays were thrown onto the legs of my trousers. I could feel the warmth in their caress and I contemplated the power of the sun. I was reminded of our kayaking trip in Glacier Bay. It had been about 4pm and we had endured a day of freezing rain throughout which the sea had threatened us with waves and physically jostled us with small icebergs, whilst the snow-capped peaks had glowered at us. We had finally made camp on a rocky beach with stiff joints and achingly cold hands and were about to prepare a perfunctory meal on the gas burner when the cloud broke above the mountain to our right. A minute later the sun burst through and the warmth that flooded down was manna from heaven. I knew at that point why early mankind had worshipped the sun.

I can easily see how the sun could become the focus of a religion. The sun is a miraculous thing, upon which people are reliant and which, thousands of years ago, was a difficult thing to explain. It would make sense to pray to it and to ask it to come back tomorrow. The ancient Egyptians worshipped the sun, as did the Aztecs and other tribes of central and South America. The Celtic Pagans in Britain and Europe also had a belief system based around the sun and the changing of the seasons, which to me, as someone who loves to experience the changing seasons, makes absolute sense.

There were eight festivals throughout the Pagan calendar, which meant you only had to wait about six weeks before the next big social knees up. The four main celebrations were based around the activities of the sun. There was the summer's longest day, when people celebrated the power of the sun. Conversely, there was the shortest day, from which point on the sun would grow in strength, bringing the world through and out of winter and was thus a day worthy of celebrating. Between these two days were the equinoxes, the mid-way points, when day and night were of equal length. At the spring equinox the crops were planted and the power of the sun was increasing and at the autumnal equinox the completion of all the harvests was celebrated as people prepared for winter.

The Pagans had become farmers and the other four celebrations had strong links to the farming calendar and were lunar festivals inserted between those of the sun. So after the shortest day, there was Imbolc in February. This roughly meant 'in-body' and was a reference to the pregnancy of the sheep which where near-term and about to bring forth new life. After the vernal equinox was Beltane on the first of May when the cattle, which had been inside shelters for the winter, were put back out to pasture. They were first passed through the smoke of purification fires to rid them of accumulated parasites.

After mid-summer came Lughnasadh, when the first of the harvests for both people and livestock were celebrated. Following the Autumnal equinox the next festival was Samhuinn. This was a celebration from 31st of October to the 2nd of November and at this time those animals that couldn't be supported for the coming winter were killed and salted. It was a time when normal roles were forgotten and people swapped jobs and played tricks on each other, a time remembered now by our modern 'trick or treat'. For the druids it was a time when the spirit world and our world came close together and some spirits would pass from one to another. Samhuinn would become in time, Halloween. For the Pagans it made sense that as the seasons followed a cyclical pattern then so should our lives. When people died their souls joined the spirit world, only to be reborn in the future.

To the Nootka Indians of the Pacific Northwest dead men were thought to be reincarnated as wolves. This fact is celebrated in the Nootkan Winter Ceremonial, the Wolf Dance. In the dance a man meets some wolves who show him how to rejuvenate the dead by singing their magical songs. The subject they bring back to life is a man, but he can take the shape of a wolf by wearing a wolf coat.

Of all the animals the wolf, respected because of its hunting prowess, had the strongest supernatural powers. Wolves were often sought after by hunters who requested their help as spirit aides. The

Kwakiutl Indians considered wolves as their ancestors. Perhaps surprisingly to those of European descent, the wolf and its spirit were seen as harmless, but the innocuous owl was greatly feared, as it was associated with the spirits of the recently dead.

    The last of the sun was gone and the gloom gathered quickly, held away from us by the fire. As I collected the detritus of our meal in order to wash up and then walked away from the fire, I felt as if a warm duvet had been ripped off me, leaving my flesh exposed in a cold room. Reluctantly I trudged the hundred or so metres down to the river to once more do battle with freezing water and pans filled with spot-welded food.

Chapter Five

Absolute stillness. I couldn't hear anything. Gary was buried in his sleeping bag and so the clamour of his respiration was muted. I moved my arm in an explosion of nylon and felt a blast of hot air rise out of my bag and past my face. The exiting heat was replaced with a swirling torrent of icy tendrils. I checked my watch, 5.45am, and then I resisted moving again to avoid any more insidious air movements.

I lay on my back listening. I was hoping with every fibre of my being that I would hear a wolf howl. There is nothing like it. The wolf has been with us for tens of thousands of years and for a large swathe of humanity in the Northern Hemisphere it has been an integral part of life. I'm sure I feel so emotive at the sound of a wolf because it triggers the most ancient parts of my brain, those bits that existed before conscious thought evolved, that relied on responding to stimuli emotionally before logic and reason had taken over. The wolf was all but exterminated in the nineteenth and twentieth centuries and its loss changed the environment in ways we could never have envisioned. Thankfully there is now a movement to protect and reintroduce wolves to their former ranges and in 1995 wolves were reintroduced to Yellowstone National Park.

It was said by some that the return of the wolf would have a devastating impact on the resident elk. However, it seems that elk numbers have remained more or less the same, but there has been an improvement in biodiversity as a result of the change in elk behaviour. Without wolves the elk were loafing on riverbanks where access to water was easy and where there was abundant lush vegetation. However, this excessive grazing was preventing the regeneration of trees such as willows and cottonwoods whose days were becoming numbered. Huge areas of the riverbank were denuded of cover, which is vital for many animals such as nesting birds.

When the wolf returned it was no longer safe for elk to lounge around rivers and so trees recovered, as did other riparian vegetation and so beavers returned and built dams and created wetlands, which hugely increased biodiversity. Who had thought that reintroducing the wolf would improve the lot of a myriad of creatures including the beaver and increase the nesting success of warblers? Unfortunately, we humans are arrogant enough to think that we understand ecosystems, but in reality we are pathetically well short of such insight.

In my sleeping bag the silence remained complete and I got to grips with thoughts of getting up. I finally stopped prevaricating, bit the bullet and made a move. Outside a thick mist hung over the surface of the river in the distance. I walked down to the river's edge in silence, confident that the land here on the gravel island was so open that I could see far enough not to startle a bear. It was as if I was the only person on the planet. The beauty I could see was purely mine. Two immature bald eagles flew towards me from the direction we had come yesterday. They gradually took shape from the mist and languidly flapped through the silky-grey vapour, their passing marked briefly by the shhhushing of their wings.

I brushed my teeth and spat a glob of toothpaste into the river to watch it float away where its scent wouldn't attract a bear. As it slowly swirled downstream I thought it had a long way to go to reach the Bering Sea and I momentarily pondered what that journey would be like.

On the way back to the tent I passed Gary ambling down to brush his teeth and while he was gone I gathered up some wood for a breakfast fire. When I couldn't find enough small twigs amongst the gravel I resorted to kicking small limbs from the bodies of the driftwood trees. The breaking wood sounded like rifle shots in the morning air. We would start this day with a thick cheese and broccoli soup and the obligatory brew made on a warming blaze.

Whilst I stirred the soup, relishing the warmth of the fire on my arms and legs, Gary studied our guidebook.

"It's a bit difficult to tell exactly where we are, but I reckon we are about here," he showed me a black Biro circle he had drawn around a collection of islands on the map.

"I reckon we did about thirty miles yesterday."

"Let's have a squiz," I said, putting my hand out for the book and Gary handed it over.

I put the soup into the coals at the edge of the fire and flicked through the maps of the guidebook. I did a bit of calculating. This was to be our fourth day on the river, albeit that our first had been a half-day. We should reach the Yukon today, meaning that to travel the 115 miles of the Teslin we had needed four and a half days. It was now Tuesday and we needed to catch the bus in Carmacks on Friday. We would have three days to cover another 110miles.

That would have worried me if we hadn't been on the Yukon before, but our experience of the swiftness of river in '97 calmed me.

Still, I was aware that we couldn't spend too much time messing about. I handed the book back to Gary and poured out the soup.

"How's your arm?" I asked as I waited for it to cool enough to eat.

"Still sore. I've taken some ibuprofen, but I've still got limited movement."

"You gonna get it looked at in Dawson?"

"Well, that could be tricky. I was looking in the book," said Gary, referring to the Alaska~Yukon Handbook by Deke Castleman and Don Pitcher, which was our bible, "and it seems there's no hospital in Dawson and I don't think there's even a clinic. I think if you're ill you go to Whitehorse."

"Shit."

I blew on my soup and let the ramifications of that information settle into my brain. If Gary had to travel back to Whitehorse to get his arm put in a cast, then the trip on the Dempster would be off, unless I did it alone. I felt a gloom descend. We ate our soup in silence, leaving the implications of a hospital visit unspoken.

I collected the bowls and cutlery and crunched off down the gravel into the mist to wash up. The river was icy and back at the fire I warmed my fingers up in my armpits and then we began loading up the canoe. We were on the water by 8am even though the mist had still not cleared. I watched it settle on the fabric of my gloves, sequining them in silvery droplets. The world was still. Absolutely and completely.

We were canoeing close to the bank on our right and although the river had narrowed again the mist made the left bank virtually invisible. I stared intently ahead watching as trees and rocks emerged from the swirling vapour.

Suddenly it was there, a massive grizzly. Head held low, sniffing the ground. It stood sideways on to us, so that I could see the hunched, powerful shoulders, his forelegs curiously long so that his back sloped downwards to his hips. Gary and I stopped paddling in unison on seeing the bear. For a long second it was unaware of our gliding approach and I hardly dared to blink as I tried to soak up the scene; The swirling river, the mist, the drizzle, the cold air, the dark forest and the bear. It took a step forward and then our movement on the river caught the corner of its eye and it looked straight at us. We weren't close enough to exchange a look exactly, although perhaps we may have been but for the mist. For the length of a heartbeat I was connected to that bear and he was the centre of my universe, and I his. Startled by the object on the river he bolted and ran up from the shoreline in an explosion of water and into the trees with the crash of whipping branches. Through the mist, watching his loping run, I saw the Sasquatch, or Bigfoot. He crashed through the undergrowth like a battle tank in a tree nursery and I could sense his shuddering power from the reaction of the trees. The mist swirled into the vacuum he had left behind and in a second it was if he had never been there. The river swept us on uninterrupted and unconcerned by such thrilling encounters.

Gradually the mist lifted and the drizzle ceased and a watery sun struggled into the sky above the forest, turning the river into platinum. A wind came up from nowhere, rippling the surface and pushing into my face. This was in conjunction with a near perfect lack of current in the river. This was the situation I had feared and I hoped upon hope that it wouldn't last long. I had to work hard to keep up some momentum. I could feel a strain in my left bicep, which was the arm at the bottom of my paddle pulling it back against the water. I stopped briefly to give it a rest and I watched the shore closely. *Were we going backwards? Possibly. Bloody hell.*

"You okay?" Gary asked.

"Yeah, no worries. Just having a rest."

At ten am. after an infinitely long battle with the wind, which in real time had been less than two hours, a tiny sandy beach beckoned to us from the right hand shore. I could make out the remains of a log cabin and we knew that this was Masons Landing. We beached the canoe and pulled it up onto the wet sand. The aspens whispered to us with a softly crackling breath as we shed our life jackets and rooted cameras out of our bags. As we entered the cathedral silence amongst the trees our bear scaring shouts were thrown back at us with a startling clarity.

All that remained of the beachfront cabin were four walls, the roof having collapsed. Amongst the forest of pine, aspen and cottonwood the remains of several other cabins hunkered silently senescing and settling back into the earth. Though their roofs had collapsed, doorways gaped wide open and glass-less windows looked out into the woods like forlorn eyes, they were somehow all the more captivating. The sun was now in the ascendancy and shafts of light pierced the canopy to spotlight bright scarlet blazes of fireweed and green sponges of moss. These startling colours were enhanced further by their backdrop of the shady pines.

Nestled amongst the timbers of a rotting cabin wall were some large mushrooms. Their skins were a brown-tinged white, the light skidding off their surfaces, deflected by a sheen of moisture. I touched one and it felt as I had expected, rubbery and cold. Although they weren't particularly attractive like the fireweed and they conjured up connotations of death, they were a reminder of the continuance of life and that the dead are recycled for the forest's renewal.

The settlement had been established at this point on the river as this had been the top of the navigable section coming upstream from the Yukon. The incoming supplies for the Livingstone goldfields were unloaded here for the 14-mile journey inland by wagon road. W.L. Mason had arrived here on July 21st 1899 with Mrs. Mason, Hazel Mason and George F. Pope. Nothing is really known about these people now, but they had come from Detroit, Michigan, presumably chasing the same dreams of gold that had afflicted so many others. They stayed here for several years and the settlement took their name. I tried to imagine living here permanently in such tiny cabins, remote from the rest of the world and enduring long winters with crushing temperatures. I felt humbled by the fortitude of those people. Nobody has lived here now since the 1930's.

Nearby Livingstone lay on Livingstone Creek, a tributary of South Fork Big Salmon, itself a tributary of Big Salmon River which merges with the Yukon 125 miles downstream of Whitehorse. Some lucky prospector had filed a discovery claim on Livingstone creek. In those days under the Placer Mining Act ordinary claims on a creek were limited to stretches of 500 feet. However, the first 'discovery claim' was given a length of 1500 feet. Even this to me seems a paltry distance, but the Livingstone discovery claim produced almost four thousand ounces of gold, which at today's prices would have been worth almost 2 million dollars!

Whilst walking around the cabins and taking photographs we split up. As I mooched about I came across an overgrown track between the trees. I could no longer see or hear Gary, although I was sure that if I spoke he would hear me. I looked down the track wondering where it went; probably Livingstone as there was a good chance this was the remains of the wagon road. I decided to follow it for a short distance, perhaps it might open out over a view or into an interesting glade. The ground was soft underfoot, dense up to shin height with regenerating trees. The sky above me was bright but down here in this arboreal city canyon the foliage had stolen most of the light.

I stood still for a second and the air was so cool and so still it felt glass-like, as if by pushing through it I might shatter it. I walked around fifty metres and then stopped, nervous all of a sudden. What if I lost the trail? What if I walked into a bear? I didn't clap, not wanting to break the spell of the silence, but I turned around and came back, the hair on my neck standing up as the ghosts of prospectors from a hundred years ago watched me leave.

Back at the cabins I saw Gary moving his tripod around. I walked back out onto the beach to wait for him to finish. I lay down on the sand looking up into the canopy of an aspen. The sunlight was reflecting off the river and dancing smoothly on the undersides of the leaves. I watched for a few minutes and then sat up, the cold having seeped from the sand into my back.

Small white bubble rafts were drifting by on the river. I remember seeing huge patches of bubbly foam near a waterfall once and was puzzled as to what the source of the pollution was. I had assumed that there was detergent in the water, but that was not necessarily the case. As plants decay they release the lipids (fats) in their cell walls and these can end up in the watercourse. Lipids are molecules comprising a hydrophilic (water loving) head and a hydrophobic (water hating) tail. When a group of lipids collect on water they raft together with their tails in the air. If they get stirred up in a waterfall or by waves they make little balls with their hydrophobic tails on the inside away from the water and like this they clump together to form a foam. These tiny bubbly rafts on the Teslin, I was convinced, were nothing sinister.

We were at Mason's Landing for about half an hour and then we continued our journey, the sandy beach releasing our canoe with a reluctant sigh. Two ravens eyed us from a gravel bank, indigo suits shining in the sunlight. As we approached too close for their comfort they took off in unison, gracefully slicing through the air like otters in a river. They arced upwards to a pine which bowed out over the river as if its trunk was made of plasticine. Already perched there were two bald eagles about ten feet apart. They watched the approaching ravens with curiosity and accepted their arrival without comment. The two newcomers sat to the landward side of their bigger brethren. As if in a show of bravado one raven puffed out its chest and dipped its head rhythmically to call out a series of crow-like 'crawws'. Its partner burbled in agreement. We cruised silently beneath all four birds who seemed to stoically ignore us. I felt honoured to be so close to such magnificent creatures.

The current in the river was still virtually non existent and I had to work with each paddle stroke to make progress, especially when the river turned into the wind which was now blowing with force enough to move the tops of the pines in lazy circles. The wind brought with it the faint smell of smoke from a distant forest fire. At least we hoped it was distant. I was uneasy for the half an hour that the smell lingered, fearing that we might paddle into an inferno. A huge red salmon jumped in front of the boat bringing my thoughts away from forest fire and as the ripples of its departure were left in our wake I realized that we had also left behind the smoke.

Up ahead I could see a black bear on the shore. I heard Gary's paddle slicing an arc in the water behind me, turning the canoe shoreward, a sure sign that he too had seen the bear. We sneaked closer as the bear wandered right to the waterline and stared into the river, still unaware of our approach. Behind it, a tangle of willow scrub shaded it from the sun, but a golden light warmed the pines standing proud of the willows.

The bear turned towards us and seemed to look straight at us. I took a photo, even though we were still over two-hundred metres away, anticipating the animal to dash into the trees. But the bear was unconcerned and it started to amble upstream along the shore, its huge forepaws flopping forward with each rolling step, its brown muzzle only inches from the gravel. The shutter of Gary's camera whirred behind me, but still, onward came the bear. We were now only a hundred metres apart and closing fast. Even without the direct sunshine I could see the sheen on the bear's coat. I thought briefly of meeting a park ranger in Glacier Bay National Park in Alaska. We were discussing the bear sightings we had had and he said to us that people would often asked him,

"How do you tell a black bear from a brown bear?"

He said he told them,

"If you're being chased by a bear and you climb a tree, but the bear follows you and kills you, it was a black bear. If you're being chased by a bear and you climb a tree but the bear pushes the tree over and then kills you, then it was a brown bear."

Sure enough this bear was smaller than the grizzly we had seen earlier in the morning. It now lifted its head, saw us and raced into the willows. I tried to get one more shot as the bear raced into cover, but my shutter clicked on a trembling branch. I was breathless for a few moments, awed by the sight of such an animal. It was thrilling to see a bear whilst on the water, but I was nervous about the possibility of meeting one while on land in camp. We had encountered a brown bear whilst hiking on land in Glacier Bay, but that had been in a treeless landscape at the foot of a glacier. We had spotted the bear over two hundred metres away, its dark shape highlighted against the blue of the glacial ice and we had backed off before it had even noticed us. Even then I had been healthily wary in a way which could possibly have been described as scared shitless! I would not like to run into a bear, up close, in the woods.

After another lunch of cheese sandwiches the river picked up speed as it gathered itself to meet the Yukon. Approaching the confluence the hills drew back and the river seemed to grow to huge proportions. The banks were again hidden behind lush carpets of grass and islands broke up the channel. Where the two rivers meet there is a small abandoned settlement known as Hootalinqua.

Hootalinqua is at the end of the Thirty-Mile stretch of the Yukon. When we had paddled past this point on the Yukon seven years previously the confluence had looked quite small, but from on the Teslin there seemed to be a vast expanse of water in front of us. We were merging from the Right Bank of the Yukon and Hootalinqua was on the left. It seemed a long way away as the racing waters of the Yukon swallowed the slow flowing water of the Teslin beneath us. The Teslin's water looked black in comparison to the blue-grey of the Yukon, which already, so close to its source, carried a heavy load of silt.

The speed of the Yukon was dizzying and it was unnervingly large. The water swirled with bubbling upwellings that broke the surface in huge flat discs that mercifully didn't rock the boat. We flirted briefly with the idea of making shore at Hootalinqua, but the speed of the river and the effort it would have required to cross put me off and we opted to go with the flow.

A Northwest Mounted Police post was built at Hootalinqua in 1898, which later also became the telegraph station. This allowed traffic on both the Yukon and Teslin rivers to be monitored. Some work has been done to restore this and another cabin on the shore, but from our position on the river we could only remember them as we raced by. Nobody has lived here since the late 1910's.

The Yukon screnaded us with its rasping hiss caused by the friction of silt particles passing along the hull of the canoe. In abandoning our attempts to cross the confluence to Hootalinqua we were swept to the right side of Shipyard Island. The island was densely covered with pine and we stopped paddling and simply stared in amongst the silent sanctuary of the trees as we rushed by. Suddenly a clearing was visible and we could see the huge wreck of a boat and some information panels. Gary turned us sharply in towards shore and I paddled like a beserker to try to land before we were swept too far past. We rocked and rolled in the current, my arms and back straining against the will of the river, which as we turned perpendicular to the flow, had surged up to within inches of coming aboard with us. Then, without warning, we suddenly broke from the torrent and into a slough by the shore. We had gained such momentum that we crashed against the pebbles of the beach.

I jumped ashore with the bow rope, panting too hard to call out to the bears, and Gary clambered over the gear to follow my disembarkation over the prow. I stopped for a moment to gather my breath, bending double with my backside propped against a tree. Gary smiled at me.

"I tell you what-we came within a midges dick of capsizing as the canoe came round," he said and turned to start unloading the gear.

When we had the canoe safely ashore Gary pulled the fleece sling off over his head.

"How's it going?" I asked, nodding at his arm.

"It's okay....a bit stiff. I'll give it a rest from the sling while we're here and try and move it about a bit."

We tied the boat to a tree and walked back the few yards to the clearing. At the back of the clearing under a washed out white sky and against pines which jostled forward, competing to throw it into shade, lay the 716 ton hulk of the paddle steamer, S.S. Norcom. It was a huge behemoth, its roof collapsed and its timbers bleaching in the dry climate. Its metal chimney stood askew, stained with streaks of rust. Even with such a huge length and breadth the ship had a narrow draught so that it could navigate the river, but I could still scarcely believe that a paddle steamer could work up the power to thrash upriver against the mighty surge of the Yukon.

The ship had been built in Seattle in 1908 and named the Evelyn. It had plied the Tenana River in Alaska until it had been wrecked. Typically for northern paddle steamers the superstructure and machinery had been salvaged and were put onto a new hull in St Michaels, Alaska. It was bought by the British Yukon Navigation Company (White Pass) and registered under the name Norcom.

The section of the Yukon above this point is known as the Thirty-Mile for its length between Lake Laberge and the confluence of the Teslin. It is a narrow and dangerous section of river and in the first 40 years of the twentieth century there were about thirty-five shipwrecks there. This island was established as a shipyard to handle the emergency repairs. One or two vessels would over-winter here to be launched in the early spring. The Norcom was hauled out of the river and retired in 1931 and has never since felt the kiss of the silty Yukon.

Seeing this wreck and thinking of shipping disasters on the Thirty-Mile reminded me of a prospector know only by his first name of Casey. Casey had laboured over the Chilkoot pass before the rush of 1898. On arriving at the shores of Lake Lindemann he built a craft to take him down the Yukon. He successfully negotiated the rapids at Whitehorse, but on the benign looking stretch of the Thirty-Mile he hit a huge rock and his vessel sank with the total loss of his outfit. Undeterred he made his way back to his starting point to try again. Once more he survived the rapids at Whitehorse that would later wipe out so many and he once more entered the Thirty-Mile. There he hit the same rock with the same catastrophic result. Casey walked into a prospector's camp, picked up a gun and shot himself. From then on the rock was known as Casey's Rock, but it was subsequently blasted out of the river, as it was a hazard to paddlesteamers.

It was late afternoon now and we were both tired. Whilst Gary took some photographs of the Norcom I had a mooch around amongst the pines for a possible place to camp. Parks Canada had installed information boards detailing facts about the wreck and the island which impressed me, as I'm sure at home such expense would not have been gone to for the small numbers of people who were likely to read them. I thought the only visitors here would be canoeists like ourselves and how many of us could there be? Many of the site's potential canoeing visitors would pass by on the left of the island and so never find this place, as we had done on our last trip on the Yukon. I subsequently found out in Whitehorse that you can arrange to get here by organized trips on motor launches, so perhaps these boards are relatively well read. Parks Canada (the equivalent to our National Park Service) had also installed long-drop, or pit toilets which I found disappointing. I'm not a fan of such toilets and would rather dig my own hole and squat where nobody else has been. That's one of the questions some people asked me when I told them where we were going on holiday, 'what do you do for toilets?'

I told them, 'the same thing as the bears do, only you dig a hole with a trowel first and then burn your toilet paper (after you've wiped your bum) so as not to leave paper, which is very slow to biodegrade.'

The brush with civilization spurred us to move on. We didn't want a camp with toilets; we wanted wilderness. However, I would have put up with it had we found a really good spot for the tent, because I was knackered, the battle with the wind having taken its toll. But what really got me moving was the fact that I was conscious of achieving more mileage in the remains of the day, with the Yukon pushing me. Wearily we re-boarded the canoe and surrendered to the current. The river was flat and wide with steep banks from which we couldn't exit. We passed below a high cliff of grey-white clay above which, an eagle circled lazily, head tilting this way and that, searching for whatever eagles search for.

I was longing for a rest by the time we spotted a small area of gravel that offered the hope of landing. Though only a few square metres in size we headed for it as if it were a runway at Heathrow. The camp it led to was perfect. It was flat as a table and elevated three or four metres above the river. I pitched the tent in a tight space between some spruce whilst Gary prepared a fire in a dining area with a view of the river.

In the light of the flames from our campfire I re-read the pages of my diary, charting our journey thus far along the Teslin. Gary sat cross-legged staring into the fire, his face lit with flickering orange and red and his mind somewhere off in deep space. How far we had come I thought, how far along the Yukon's waterways and how far through life. We had come a long way indeed since camping in Gary's back garden and exploring the woods of the Leven River as young teenagers. We had grown up perhaps, but we had lost none of our sense of adventure or wonder. I felt pleased with that thought. The excitement we felt now at seeing bears and eagles was exactly the same as that we had felt on seeing our first deer.

As teenagers our woods had held a thrill for us knowing from their tracks and shed antlers that deer were there and our eventual encounter was breathtaking. I still walk along that riverbank with the same sense of anticipation. I often revisit the Leven in the spring and early summer, the time when as boys we would venture out again on our bicycles after the confinement of winter.

The track to my favourite spot follows a field edge, the river on my right, some ten feet below me, the field on the left intermittently occupied by sheep. At that time of year the steep banks are crowded with the white umbelliferous heads of cow parsley and bumblebees, hoverflies, dragonflies, damselflies and butterflies lumber, buzz, dart, flounce and float through the air as I pass. The river is quite shallow here in places, tumbling melodically over a rocky bed and decorated with long green streamers of water crows foot.

The sun beats down on me and I begin to sweat. A deep pool in the river below looks deliciously cool, half of it in the shade of the trees on the opposite bank and half of it sparkling icily in the sun. Big trout move lazily near the surface, like myself, in no rush to be anywhere. The path moves away from the river for a short stretch and I labour uphill and into the cool embrace of some hawthorn and hazel. The air is abuzz with insects and on a hazel leaf I watch fascinated as a hoverfly is caught by a wasp. The wasp quickly bites off the head of its victim, which rolls away like a human head from a guillotine. The wasp takes off carrying the body, which it will use to feed the growing larvae in the nest.

Back on the river I hear the single-note call of a kingfisher and as I squat down amongst the cow parsley to hide it flies past, a shimmering blue dart. I settle down and wait for the return flight. The smell of liquorice wafts over me from a clump of sweet cicely near my feet where its delicate white flowers support a soldier beetle waiting patiently to ambush any insect tempted by the pollen. Its antennae wave slowly from the top of its bright red head, palpating the air for clues of its prey. Presently the kingfisher streaks past again in its rush to feed its growing young. A blackbird clatters an alarm call in its wake.

Further on I sit by the remains of an old weir and there I spot a mink. It emerges from the bushes twenty feet away, its sinuous body such a dark brown that it's almost black with a white beard under its chin. It looks at me briefly and scurries off. The mink and the Canada geese I see on the river Tees are pleasant reminders of the Yukon wilderness.

As I stand up I notice the delicate, almost diamond-shaped footprint of a red fox in the mud and a smudged deer slot only a few feet away from that. Although the ravages of man have battered Britain and its true wildernesses have been lost, there is still much beauty in the animals and plants that remain. I don't have to travel to the far side of the world to be enchanted by my fellow creatures. The river Tees and its tributaries such as the Leven have much to offer. In the glow of the fire I thought how good it is to take time out and walk with wild things, just to simply 'be' for a short time.

Chapter Six

Some time during the night there was a crash outside the tent. I had probably only been half asleep, or perhaps close to the surface in REM sleep, or perhaps I hadn't even really fallen asleep, but my mind emerged in a jumble. I was now awake as if I had just been doused in ice water. My heart was pounding and I could feel adrenaline squirting from my adrenals and into my bloodstream like quick flowing lava.

"Holy shit! Did you hear that?" Gary asked, the nylon of his sleeping bag 'shushing' as he must have sat up. His head was barely three feet from mine, yet in the pitch black I couldn't see him.

"Unfortunately I did."

"What do you think it was?"

"I don't know, but it was a big bastard, whatever it was," was my scholarly assessment as the zoologist of the expedition.

There was nothing to do now but try and calm down from the adrenaline rush. My ears strained for information but nothing was forthcoming other than my pulse. Gradually, as the seconds of silence stretched into minutes I relaxed and surrendered to sleep.

I woke up at six and kept the prevaricating over whether to get up or not to a mere ten minutes. I unzipped the top of my bag and sat up to wriggle into the fleecy jumper I had been using as a pillow. I pulled my glasses out of the pocket in the tent wall and rubbed the lenses with the bottom of my jumper knowing that if I just put them on cold they would mist up in seconds. I spun around on my bum to sit cross-legged before the door. I unzipped it and poked my legs out into the tent's atrium where I had left my boots. As my legs went out a wall of cold, damp air collapsed inward. Gary pulled his sleeping bag over his head.

"Shite," he muttered and I chuckled with malevolent glee.

With boots on I leaned forward and unzipped the flap of the flysheet and then launched myself into a swirling fog. The silence was as dense as the air. I squeezed and pushed my way through the dense, interlaced branches of the trees, my boots clumping over their string-like roots. I made my way along the top of the river cliff into the clearing where we had had our fire last night and where we had left our gear. A spruce ripped my hat off with a dexterous branch whilst its neighbour shivered and showered me with the icy water droplets it had been collecting overnight for just such an opportunity.

I retrieved fleece, trousers and coat from the storage barrel and then clapped absently, remembering last night's crash in the dark. The echo of my clap bounced around as if I had been in a cave. All but the very edge of the river was lost in the turbid air and the trees were mustered too close to see very far into the woods. 'How long have you been here?' I asked the pine next to me via telepathy. It didn't reply. I touched its bark, which was rough and cold, scabbed in patches with grey-green lichen. Unable to move and as cold as the grave it didn't 'feel' like a living being under my fingers. But living it was and I felt an affinity for this organism which would live so long, stoically withstanding the summer heat and the intense depths of the winters' cold, growing slowly and steadily into a giant. I noticed that there was a big pile of moose dung at its feet. So that had been our nocturnal interloper. How the hell had a moose squeezed in here through this thicket? Had biologists completely failed to observe the fact that moose can teleport themselves from one place to another?

Gary emerged and rummaged for his clothes.

"Moose," I said pointing at the dung.

"Uh, huh. You were right then."

"About what?"

"Big bastard."

"Oh yeah."

While the barrel was open I pulled out part of a paper shopping bag and a lighter and got started preparing a fire. 'We might as well give the fog some time to burn off' I thought.

On our return to England I gave a talk about our journey to members of some society or other and I was asked, 'If there was fog most mornings and you waited for it to clear, why not just get up later?' Well, we could have done that, but I can sleep at home and here I was, up and about in an amazing wilderness. Why pass up the chance to experience it by staying in bed? How often can we have the luxury of watching a new day emerge at home? The flames licked greedily at the paper and we soon had a pot in the fire boiling water for tea.

We were on the water by 7.30am, impatient to go, even though the air had still not cleared. The river had narrowed although it was difficult to gauge its dimensions as the fog prevented us from seeing both banks at the same time. In the dim light the grey waters had turned to milk and the world was mysterious and ethereal. It was akin to being in space, as the silence was so profound it could only have been matched in the vacuum of the universe. 'In the Yukon no one can hear you scream,' I thought.

The pines cut a jagged line of silhouettes, above which floated a spectral white disc masquerading as the sun. The scene had a primeval feel to it. We were in a timeless place, somewhere where the next wildlife encounter might not be a bear, but a tyrannosaur, or some other extraordinary beast.

Though we didn't see it through the vaporous air we passed by the wreck of the paddle steamer, the S.S. Klondike, lying at the foot of a huge clay cliff. We didn't even see the cliff. She had sunk here in 1936 on her way downstream to Dawson with a load of cargo and some forty passengers. Captain Charles Coghlan had just seen her through the dangerous water of the Thirty-Mile when he handed her over to first mate Malcolm McAuley. For some unknown reason the ship slipped sideways and struck a bluff. McAuley tried to correct her but she struck something else which disabled the paddlewheel. She was pulled onward by the current as water poured into her hull.

The passengers were disembarking into the lifeboats as she struck her final resting-place at the foot of the cliff. A team of horses was let out of the front hold to fend for themselves, but several cows were trapped in the rear by shifting cargo and they drowned, the only casualties of the whole incident. The telegraph station at Hootalinqua was notified by clipping a 'key' into the line that ran the length of the riverbank and a river trader armed with a motor launch set off to the rescue. The Hootalinqua telegraph operator also informed Whitehorse of the incident and a float plane came up to evacuate the passengers from a makeshift camp.

During the morning the mist swirled and danced to a tune of its own. Several times it looked as if it was about to lift only for it to thicken again and clamp us in a cold, damp, writhing caress. After two and a half hours on the water it finally relented and the world was revealed to us in bright sunshine under a clear sky.

We pulled out onto a mudflat at 10.30am for a snack. We hopped around in the quagmire, striving for the grass fringing the mud which promised dryer ground. As we shifted the gear landward we spotted a perfect wolf print in the mud. 'We're still here,' it said, 'just because you haven't heard us, or seen us, we're still here, watching you.' Just the sight of that print made me buzz with excitement.

Though the sky was clear and the sun shining, it was bitterly cold. My teeth were chattering and my hands shaking as I buttered crackers and sliced cheese for our snack. If I could have done it with my gloves on I would have. Today was the first of September and the last of the summer had definitely been wrung from the air. I stopped my teeth clacking long enough to eat my crackers and then we were back on the river and I was gratefully paddling to keep warm.

We passed several areas where there had been forest fires. The pines were blackened sticks, some of them teetering at odd angles like dragons' teeth. We could estimate the relative age of the burns by the regeneration that was taking place. Amongst the black sticks bright flares of yellow and gold waved at us where birch, aspen and cottonwoods had taken hold. In older areas the colours became denser and the greens of pines had started to return. A young male moose stared at us with an accusing look as we passed it amongst a burn. It seemed to be laying the blame for the devastation at our feet and although it hadn't identified the right individuals, it probably wasn't wrong about the species. I could almost hear him 'tut' as we left him behind.

The river had widened a little and up ahead we could see Big Salmon Village. This was an abandoned village at the confluence of the Yukon and Big Salmon River. During the month of June the Big Salmon floods and ploughs into the Yukon as a big, fast flowing stream fed by meltwater, but by this time of year it has faded to a trickle and the shore in front of the village is a shallow gravel bed.

As we approach Big Salmon I remembered reaching this point in 1997. Before we had actually seen the confluence we had heard the sound of a motor launch approaching. After several days in the wilderness it was an unusual and an irritating noise. It whined louder and appeared from around a bend, its nose high in the water pushing a bow wave and wake out to the sides as it bulled its way through the current. At first I thought it was passing traffic, but then it soon became apparent that it was approaching us deliberately. I began to get anxious, nervous of the wake, which was ploughing through the water towards us like the back of a monstrous anaconda.

The boat slowed and the ranger piloting it called out to us asking that we stop at Big Salmon to fill in a backcountry questionnaire. We turned the canoe to point into the wash as it snaked under us and gave us a shake. His mission complete, the ranger turned the boat away from us and whined off back to the village. I felt resentful of the mechanized intrusion into our journey.

We finally waded ashore only to find the 'abandoned village' a virtual hippie commune. Several of the old cabins seemed to be occupied and the amount of gear scattered about indicated that people were living here the length of the summer. We were intercepted by the park ranger as we got back to our canoe.

"Hi guys," he said cheerfully. "Where are you from?"

"The north-east of England."

"Oh really. Whereabouts?"

"Middlesbrough," I said.

"Middlefurrow?"

"No, Middlesbrough."

"Middleruff?" he tried again, obviously struggling with my accent.

"No Middlesbrough. It's near Newcastle," I said.

He was still none the wiser, so I just told him we were on the border with Scotland. I didn't have the patience for a conversation because I was still pissed off with him for driving a motorboat at us.

"Oh, okay."

He handed over the questionnaire, which asked about our experiences and wildlife encounters. Whilst we filled them in he looked over our gear.

"You guys got a gun?" he asked.

"Nope," Gary said.

"A bear spray?"

"Nope," I said.

At that he looked at us with incredulity on his face. His expression clearly said, *what kind of numbnuts comes out here without a gun or a bear spray.*

I just smiled at him and went back to the form. I got to a question that asked something along the lines of 'what would have enhanced your visit?' I was tempted to put something about an absence of rangers in motor boats, but I resisted, after all, this guy might be rescuing us in few days.

This year, wanting to avoid the crowds, we kept to the left bank of the Yukon and gave Big Salmon Village a wide berth. The tributary itself slid by almost unnoticed. In the local Tutchone dialect the river had been called Gy Cho Ch, meaning literally, salmon-big-water. George Dawson, senior officer with the Yukon Expedition for the department of the interior in the late 1880's, for whom Dawson City is named, used this English translation of the Tutchone as the name for the river.

Just beyond Big Salmon Village we pulled over on the opposite side of the Yukon to have our lunch. It was midday and the sky was blue, but we noticed for the first time that the sun had barely climbed half way into the sky and it was surrounded by a thin halo. There seemed to be no heat from the sun whatsoever. We were indeed now approaching some northerly latitudes and the river was heading even further north.

As we sat finishing our lunch there was a commotion in the sky, the distinctive barking and honking of a flock of geese. I stood up and scanned the heavens. Suddenly there they were, two loose V's of rhythmically flapping Canada geese. Slowly, as the whole flock moved, individuals would drift closer or away from the rest only to drift back to position as if drawn by a magnet, their wings, bodies and necks moving sinuously whilst their heads remained stock still. I smiled at the sight of them and at the sound of their exuberant camaraderie. They were heading south. How would they view us, foolishly heading north towards the onrushing winter?

Geese are amazing creatures. Bar headed geese migrate over the Himalayan Mountains where even the fittest and best acclimatized humans can only stagger without supplementary oxygen. Geese don't need to acclimatize, they can take off and reach 9000m within a day. But it's not just geese that can fly high, all birds are far better adapted to altitude than humans. They can fly where there is little oxygen because their lungs are structured differently to ours, they are proportionately smaller than ours and yet are much more efficient.

Within a bird's body, between its organs and in the skull and other bones are a series of air spaces. The anterior and posterior air spaces are linked by two tubes to form a circuit. One of those tubes has a set of fine filamentous pipes, which act as the lung. When the bird breathes in the air goes into the posterior air sacs and when it breathes out that bolus of air is forced *through* the lung. On the next inhalation the air goes into the anterior air sacs and then out of the bird's mouth on the next exhalation. Because the air passes through the lung it means that it flows continuously over the respiratory surface allowing far better gas exchange than in our simple 'in-out, blind ended, air bags'.

Although you might intuitively think that our breathing is controlled by oxygen levels in our blood, it is in fact carbon dioxide that stimulates us to breathe. This is because at sea level, where we evolved, there is far more oxygen in the air than we need, so getting oxygen isn't a problem. However, as we metabolize our food the waste product is carbon dioxide, which dissolves into carbonic acid in our blood. Allowing that to build up would be detrimental to one's health and so maintenance of carbon dioxide levels is of greater import and has a narrower margin of error. We get rid of that carbon dioxide by 'blowing it off' through our exhalations.

Birds are less sensitive to carbon dioxide than we are. So when they breathe rapidly at altitude, thus flushing carbon dioxide from their blood, they can carry on breathing where we would stop to allow carbon dioxide to build back up. Birds also have proportionately larger hearts than we do, pushing blood around their tissues more effectively.

The sight of the geese in flight made me catch my breath. They flew over, their shadows racing by my feet and their voices ringing in my ears. Their barrel chests seemed too large for flight, held aloft as they were by rapid, shallow beats of wings seemingly too small for the task. As they passed over I got a good view of their white rumps, the 'tail lights' by which they could follow each other in bad weather. I silently wished them a good journey.

Not far beyond Big Salmon Village the river opened out again and became littered with islands, but unlike the Teslin, there were no shallows to avoid and we could choose our route without fear of grounding. Up ahead a grizzly was looking into the river. It hadn't seen us and as we sped towards it it waded out and began swimming. With its head above water its ears were highlighted as those of a classic teddy bear. How an animal could swim in this current I didn't know. I was damn sure that if I had set out to cross I would have been swept miles down river and may possibly never have made the far side, but the bear powered out unconcerned. It had gone perhaps twenty metres when it spotted us and did a swift U-turn, the morning ablutions ruined. It clambered ashore as we drifted by. Its fur, with the exception of its head and neck was matted down with water and it shook itself like a dog, flinging a silver spray into the sunlight and recovering its shaggy pelage. It watched us pass with some disdain and then retreated into the willows.

Ten miles or so beyond Big Salmon we kept our eyes open for the remains of Cyr's dredge, of which Gary wanted a photo. The approach to the neck of land on which the dredge sits was confusing. The river was huge and there were some big islands and lots of smaller gravel bars. In '97 we had cruised past here without finding it and I was fairly sure we would do the same again. The sun was shining brightly and the river glittered. I had stripped down to a T-shirt and had even started to sweat beneath my life jacket. I thought about putting my sunglasses on, but dismissed the idea, as it would surely bring clouds racing in like crows to a road-kill.

By a fluke, which Gary insisted was in fact his brilliant navigating, we came across an information board exclaiming the location of the dredge. We pulled ashore and he stalked off to look for the dredge itself. I waited with the boat, uninterested in old machinery. I stood up on the pebbles of the shore and stretched my legs and back. Two ravens squabbled raucously on a nearby gravel bar, hopping and leaping at each other with outstretched wings. Although I couldn't hope to understand their language the sound of their voices was both amusing and soothing.

I took my life jacket off and pulled the canoe onto the firm grip of the beach. I turned my back to the sun and felt its rays massage my shoulders. I turned back to the ravens just in time to see a peregrine falcon stoop out of the sky and bomb them. The ravens ducked low to the ground and the peregrine missed them, pulled up and raced off in a level flight into the pines on the far shore. The ravens continued their squabble as if nothing had happened. I think that perhaps it had been a half-hearted attempt by the falcon, as if it had seen the ravens and thought, 'well it would be rude not to have a go'. But the risk of bombing a bird on the ground is great. If it went in committed and missed, it would crash into unforgiving ground. A stoop on a bird in flight, its usual method of hunting, allows the luxury of a safe miss.

Cyr's dredge had been built by Laurent Cyr and Boyd Gordon. It was a big piece of machinery. It was twenty-three feet wide and thirty-two feet long with a hull depth of thirty-three inches. It had had a boom loaded with twenty buckets capable of gouging down into the riverbed fourteen feet below the waterline. It had been built in 1940 and had cost the two men $10,000 to build. In the end it had operated for only twenty-three days. In that time they managed to recover about $2,000 worth of gold, but they had got here too late in the season. With the water beginning to freeze they had beached the dredge with the intention of returning the following summer. They never returned, I presume because of the intervention of World War Two, but I don't know. I wondered what had happened to them.

A movement at my feet interrupted my thoughts. Some tiny fish had darted into the shallows. As I bent down to examine them they sped away, back into the river. Now that I was squatting by the water I turned over a stone to see if there was anything lurking beneath. On the Leven I would almost certainly have been rewarded with a scuttling twin-tailed stonefly nymph or a mayfly nymph with its characteristic three 'tails.' I might have unearthed a caddis fly, lumbering around in a case made of pebbles or twigs. But, there was nothing. Nothing under the next two stones either. They were river-smooth and slick with algae, but otherwise devoid of life. I was sure I had just been unlucky, but the water was too cold to turn over more stones and besides Gary returned from his foray amongst the scrub.

"Any good?" I asked.

"Nowt special," he said with a shrug.

I was glad I had enjoyed the sun and the ravens instead.

Half an hour later we made shore looking to camp at a place on our map marked as Erickson's Wood Camp. It was hard to spot the exact place to land as at this point the Yukon was fringed with a high river cliff. We landed amongst the rocks and boulders at the waterline and scrambled up the sandy cliff. We had stopped too early and the vegetation was impenetrable, so we re-boarded and floated another 200-metres downstream.

By the time we had hauled the gear into camp and the canoe up the cliff and out of reach of the river we were sweating heavily and it wasn't just from the work. From nowhere the sun seemed to have found new resolve and was baking the earth in the last of the afternoon. Small explosions of dust erupted with my footsteps over the dry ground.

This was an absolutely perfect camp. From our raised terrace we looked down on the milky blue water of the Yukon racing by with its characteristic 'boiling' surface. The hills opposite us were an autumnal riot of colour, as there seemed to be a high proportion of deciduous trees amongst the pine. A gentle breeze blew through camp filling the air with the cottony seeds of fireweed and making the aspens whisper.

The boiling appearance of the river was due to a combination of its speed and a rocky bed. As the water surges over a large rock on the bottom a partial vacuum is created on the downstream side of the boulder as the water rips away from it. The implosion of this rising bubble causes the roiling at the surface. When we first saw the Yukon in Whitehorse in 1997, we were horrified. We had come out having never been in canoes before. We had thought, 'we've been in kayaks, how hard can it be?'

We had read that the river had been used by paddle steamers such as the SS Klondike and so we had inferred from that that the river must be fairly placid. As we strolled into Whitehorse from the campground we went into a Parks Canada information centre to see a map of the river with rapids marked on. Rapids! We had not expected rapids. How the hell did paddle steamers get up rapids? What we hadn't known was that at places such as Five Finger Rapids, there were iron rings attached to the cliff walls. To these were attached a cable which ran back to a winch on the deck of the steamer. The steamers thus pulled themselves up the rapids. Despite our fears we had survived, the canoe gliding gracefully over the 'boily bits' and the rapids turned out to be worse in our minds than in reality.

There was a small log cabin at Erickson's wood camp with the regulation collapsed roof, set back from the river in a clearing. Wood camps like this had spread along the Yukon in the early 1900's to feed the boilers of the paddle steamers. Prior to 1936 this one had been known as Byers camp, but when Byer had died the Erickson brothers who had worked for him took over. The Erickson's weren't here long, as by the late 1940's someone else had taken over, but theirs was the name that had stuck.

We both took photographs looking up into the canopies of a group of seven aspens whose trunks and leaves provided a wonderful contrast to the blue sky above. Whilst we were doing this a chipmunk busied itself collecting berries from a bush nearby and we soon moved on to trying to capture him on film. He was an awkward customer to catch on film because it was only every few minutes that he appeared either from behind the leaves of the bush, or out from the long grass. I took a couple of shots and retired in frustration, but Gary, the consummate professional, persevered and got some good shots.

I sloped quietly away, leaving Gary hunched over his camera and settled down, propped up on a log and a life preserver, to write an entry in my diary. In the warm air I had shed my hiking boots for sandals and felt warm enough to just wear a T-shirt with no fleece. This was easily the warmest the weather had been so far and it proved to be the warmest it would be for the rest of our trip.

A mosquito landed on my arm and stabbed me. I brushed it off only to have another one whine piercingly around my ear. I got up and stalked off to root through my stuff for some repellent. Part of the reason we had chosen to come this late in the season was that there would have been the first frosts which would have killed many of the biting insects, but here on a warm afternoon there were obviously survivors. If you sit in one spot for long enough they will track you down. Mosquitoes are very sensitive to the carbon dioxide animals breathe out and they also home in on body heat. Sitting and writing my diary I had been a hot and gassy beacon.

It's only the females who suck your blood. The males live peaceable lives drinking nectar from flowers, but the females need blood to nourish their eggs. Drinking blood is a tricky business, not only is it difficult to get to, but the 'donor' is often likely to object. The mouth of a mosquito is like a sharp drinking straw through which it sucks up fluid, but being so tiny, our blood, filled as it is with giant red blood cells, is extremely thick. Dragging blood out of a person is comparable to us trying to suck a really thick milkshake up a straw. But whilst we have all the time in the world to quaff a milkshake, a mozzie is under pressure because the victim may take potentially lethal retaliatory action. So, to help things along, mosquitoes have air spaces in their head and by flexing some muscles they can alter the shape of them, causing a partial vacuum in their head and thus pulling up blood. They also pump some anti-coagulants into you, which is what reacts causing the bites to itch after the mozzie has gone. All in all they're devious little bastards.

Later in the afternoon as the sun went down, the woods were bathed in a glorious golden light and the airborne fireweed seeds became glowing forest sprites. As the air cooled we donned our fleeces and settled in by a driftwood campfire to watch the demise of the sun. Later, with food in our bellies and a cup of tea in hand we stared at the flames like Buddhist priests trying to contemplate the meaning of life. The flames danced and flickered in yellow and red tongues, devouring greedily the bone-dry wood. I poked some unburned branches towards the centre of the fire with a long stick and then held it in the flames to burn until the tip fell off like the ash from an untended cigarette. The fire was much better entertainment than a TV.

Gary had been studying the maps in our river guide while I played with the fire.

"I reckon we've done 43 miles today," he announced and I nodded my acknowledgement.

The current in the Yukon had made a huge difference to our speed as we had hoped.

"We'll see the Highway tomorrow."

The highway he was referring to was the Robert Campbell Highway, which ran from Watson Lake to Carmacks. We were approaching Carmacks and from tomorrow we expected to start seeing other signs of Humanity, as day-trippers from there would come upriver in powerboats. I savoured our solitude as best I could.

I took the guidebook from Gary and peered at the maps in it in the flickering light. As best as I could tell from the map in front of me and the map in my memory, tomorrow we would be passing part of the route of the Yukon Quest Dog Sled Race, which joins the left bank on the way into Carmacks. This race is held every year in February and run on a 1025mile route between Whitehorse in the Yukon Territory and Fairbanks, Alaska. It is one of the two great dog sled races of the world, the other being the Iditarod, run in March between Anchorage and Nome.

I liked the idea of running behind a team of dogs in the wilderness, but I have neither the dedication to raise and train the dogs, nor the skills needed to survive a race in temperatures that can plunge to minus 50, when the slightest mistake can mean death. One of the best books I have ever read is Gary Paulsen's, 'Winterdance', about his experience of the Iditarod. Although I will never run the Iditarod or the Quest I have had a go behind a team of dogs.

In a place called Hallingen in Norway, Melanie and I, and several others with us on a cross-country skiing holiday, had a go at dog sledding. Mel and I left the hotel at midday and scrunched our way through the snow that had fallen the night before. It squeaked as if we were walking in polystyrene chips. The sun shone with a blue-white glow on the snow and the light bounced around the white trunks of the birch forest around us.

We walked out onto an open plateau to the sound of baying dogs. There were three sledges anchored in the snow and hitched up to teams of six dogs. The dogs were huskies, a patchwork of blacks, whites, browns and greys, most of them with startlingly blue eyes. The guy whose dogs they were took the first sled, we took the second and another couple took the third. Melanie got inside the zip-up bag on the sled and I stood on the brake between the runners at the back, my hands gripping tightly onto the handlebar. The brake consisted of a metal bar with downward facing spikes which a spring lifted clear of the snow when the driver took his/her feet off it.

After giving me my instructions, which were, 'Don't overtake me'; the dogs' owner boarded his sledge and took off. I stepped off the brake and onto the runners and the dogs exploded forwards after the sledge in front. It was incredible. There were only six dogs, small ones at that in comparison to my German shepherd, but if I hadn't had a tight grip, the acceleration would have pitched me off onto my ass. What, I thought to myself, must it be like with a full team of twelve dogs.

With a breeze on my face carrying the sound of the dogs' breathing and pounding paws, we blasted over the snow, the runner's shushhhhing madly beneath my feet. The ground wasn't by any means flat and we lurched into and bounced out of hollows and flew from the tops of humps, the dogs totally unconcerned about the riders behind. That the dogs made no allowance for inexperienced mushers was clear from the tales we had heard from the group who had tried it this morning. More than one sled had been tipped over, or a driver thrown off. I grinned like a madman and held on as if I was hanging onto the skids of an airborne helicopter.

Norway raced by. The hills in the distance were magnificent and we passed a couple of picturesque wooden cabins and then we were into the woods. The trail switched this way and that and as we hit bumps on the turn I leaned into them to stop us going over. I was acutely aware that the runners were thinner than the width of my boots and that if I lost my footing I would be in some difficulty. I laughed out loud. This was fantastic. We sped out over a frozen lake, given away by its smoothness and by the thick stand of common reed along one edge in its regal winter brown with sagging feathery heads.

We left the lake by way of a short slope littered with boulders, of which we missed none and I was grateful that I had kept a bend in my knees to absorb the shocks. At the top, the lead team had stopped and I jumped on the brakes. Our leader explained that on the way back we should stop before this point and that he would lead the team down, as many people tended to get pitched out here. With that explained we once more hit warp speed.

Where the trail opened out into a clearing we stopped and the drivers were to change places with the passengers for the journey back. Melanie wasn't keen to drive, but there was to be no arguing.

"I've had an 80 year old lady do this. You can do it too," she was told.

We changed places and then the charge began again. Up ahead the lead team disappeared over the ledge and down onto the lake and we pelted after them. This was the point where we were supposed to stop.

"Stand on the brakes. Stand on the brakes. STAND ON THE FUCKING BRAKES!" I yelled.

"I am, I AM," shouted Mel, rising panic apparent. She just wasn't heavy enough on the brakes to slow the dogs down. At the bottom of the precipice I could see the lead team parked and our instructor leaping off and pelting through the snow in our direction, a look of fear on his face and his hands waving in a, 'didn't I tell you to wait there you daft bastards?'- kind of windmill. Too late. We were over the lip of the drop and bouncing off our first boulder before you could say 'dog shit'. We spent several seconds airborne and took several very hard knocks and to Melanie's eternal credit she hung on and kept us upright. We landed safely on the lake and tried to look casual as we skidded to a halt behind the first team. What a rush. Mel was allowed to retake her place in the sled and I got back on the runners. The whole ride only lasted about half an hour, but it was a half-hour we will never forget. Days such as this and days spent on the Yukon are days of which memories are made. The day to day of our ordinary lives is so often lost in a forgettable blur. But when you take time out to go somewhere new the different, the beautiful and the exciting are preserved for us to relive and savour and life slows down. Hopefully, when I'm old I'll have a life to remember.

Thoughts of dog sledding receded as a gust of wind waved a hot blast of air over me from the fire. The zephyr danced away and the flames returned to their vertical gyrations. I watched the coals, spellbound as they glowed red and then white and back again, the colours moving smoothly like skin shades on a moody octopus. The end of a branch that had been held above the coals suddenly slumped and sent a seething swarm of sparks skyward.

"What's the arm like?" I asked Gary, noticing he had taken the sling off.

"It's a bit sore but not too bad."

"Do reckon it was broken then?"

"Yeah I do."

"So what you gonna do. You going to hospital at Whitehorse?"

Gary stared into the fire for a few seconds, mulling it over

"Bollocks to it," Gary said suddenly. "If it doesn't get any worse I'll wait till we get home to get it looked at."

"Are you sure," I asked.

"Uh-huh."

"Good on yer," I said, my dreams of the Dempster Highway rekindled.

We sat in silence for a long time watching the flames and imagining what it might be like on the Dempster Highway where we had read that on the open tundra you could spot wolves, caribou, lynx, wolverine, moose, even musk oxen.

"How's Stan doing with that bird he was seeing?" Gary asked a few moments later, apropos of nothing.

"They've split up," I said.

"Oh, right. What happened? I thought they'd moved in together."

"Yeah, they had, but she said he was taking the piss out of her, getting her to do all his washing and ironing. So I asked him 'were you?' and he said he was."

Gary smiled to himself as he watched the flames.

"Anyway," I said, "one of his mates asked him to go to Tenerife with him and she said 'If you go to Tenerife with the lads we're finished.'"

"What'd he do?" Gary asked, smiling as he anticipated the answer.

"He went to Tenerife."

I leaned back as another gust of wind blew a constellation of sparks up into the night sky.

"When he got back she had taken all her stuff out of the flat. I asked him 'Where you gutted?' and he said 'Yeah, you should have seen how much washing I brought back from Tenerife.'"

At that Gary howled with laughter and I had to join him.

Chapter Seven

It was six o'clock in the morning and there was light enough in the tent to see by.

"Gaz?" I said.

"Yeah."

"Have you farted or has someone just parked a truck-load of shit outside?"

I couldn't see Gary's face because he had his back to me, but I could see his chest bouncing up and down as he laughed a silent laugh.

"You know, I seriously think you should see a GP when you get home because that is absolutely rank," I said.

There was more laughter, only this time it broke out audibly.

"Bollocks. I'll have to get up just to escape that."

I emerged from the tent into alpine-fresh air that for a change was mist free. I hopped down the sandy cliff to the river's edge to clean my teeth. The Yukon swirled past immutable, immense and, in comparison to the length of my puny life, permanent. Without the hull of the canoe to rasp on the water was silent save for the odd gentle splash as an eddy flopped over a stone on the bank.

On the opposite side of the river was the entrance to Erickson's slough. We had entered the slough on our last trip on the Yukon and on the far side of the narrow entrance was a lake the size of a football field. We had sneaked in there hoping to spot a moose, but we had been unlucky. The water was crystal clear and fringed with lush grasses and we had fancied a walk around the lake. Unfortunately, the ground was treacherous and as I put my boot onto what looked like solid ground it sank into deep mud and water raced in to share the hole with my boot. Our paddles had stirred up silt and particles of vegetation without even touching bottom. We had stayed a few minutes floating in the total calm and then made our way back out onto the racing Yukon.

As I stared across at the entrance to the slough, in my mind's eye I could see a moose in there, up to its shoulders in water, antlers shedding a cascade as its head came up from the bottom, water weeds dangling from its mouth. I would have to just imagine it, as there was no way we could cross the river from here, the current would take us well downstream and paddling upstream was out of the question. For the same reason we couldn't reach the slough now, we had missed this campsite seven years ago.

As I brushed my teeth I looked out over the hills, the sides of some of which were bald of timber. I looked carefully lest I catch sight of a bear or a wolf, but there was nothing except the beauty of the open hills, the variegated trees and the sky. I knew though, that the wolves and the bears were out there and that knowledge enhanced the splendour of the scene.

I clambered back up the bank and sat at the top as if I were sat on a dock, my legs dangling down in thin air. I placed my hands beneath my thighs and felt the cool of the sandy soil in my fingers. I felt now that I was a part of the landscape around me. I was seeing it, truly seeing it, with eyes of someone acutely dependent on its moods. I had felt the warmth of the sun and the chill of frost. My ears had heard the profound depths of its silence, the stirrings of the wind, the call of the raven, the chatter of a squirrel and the cry of an eagle. I had breathed in the clear air, the vaporous fog and the scent of the forest. I could feel the very skin of the landscape with my hands. I felt a deep sense of fulfilment. I remembered a poster I had seen in the shop at Whitehorse airport. It showed two people on top of a spectacular cliff looking out over the wilderness and the caption read, 'Somewhere down there is your soul-Canada's Yukon.' I felt now as if my soul was swelling, reaching out to the space around me, filling the woods and expanding into the hills and the vault of the sky. That description may seem a bit over the top, corny even, written down on paper and I'm sure some of my friends would say that I'm losing the plot, but I was deeply moved and my emotions and sense of wonder were vigorously stirred.

Gary was up and about when I walked back over to the tent. Today I felt I wanted to linger a little in camp and savour the majesty of our setting.

"Shall we have a fire and make some soup for breky while we wait for the bio-hazard to disperse?" I nodded in the direction of the tent. Gary, rummaging around in a barrel for the rest of his clothes grunted,

"Alright by me."

After breakfast we broke camp and were on the water by 8am. Incredibly, after the first bend in the river the banks drew sharply in and we were once again on a relatively small and intimate waterway. An eagle flew very close to us, its head and tail dazzlingly white in the sunlight.

Up ahead we saw the distinctive moving black lump of a black bear. It was shambling along the shore where the rocks were obviously stable, as they were interspersed with a carpet of grass. The bear took shape as we closed in, camera shutters blazing. A raven hopped out of the bruin's path and by the way the bear had moved I got the impression that it had made the raven move just out of devilment. The raven gave a weak 'Krrraaw' of protest as it flew out over the river, its wingtips going so close to the water surface, its flight so perfectly stable, that it seemed it must have been guided along on a solid rail.

As the bear disappeared into the willow scrub I rewound my film and opened up the back of the camera to change to a new one. As I did that, head down and unaware of my surroundings, Gary calmly said,

"There's another one."

I looked up to see a grizzly walking along, up to its belly in a fringe of long, lush grass.

"Shit," I cursed, my fingers suddenly acquiring the dexterity of frankfurters, as Gary laughed quietly to himself at my panic, his eye glued firmly to the viewfinder of his camera.

The bear was a beauty with a light brown muzzle and a darker face with milk chocolate shoulders and plain chocolate rump and legs. I was struck again by his, or her, teddy bear ears. The bear watched us approach for several seconds and then stood up on its rear legs to get a better view. Its huge forepaws dangled down to its thighs like large frying pans tipped with immense claws. It didn't like what it saw and ran off into the trees.

Bears are magnificent creatures. Brown bears and grizzlies are the same species though they tend to be called grizzlies over most of the continent, but are known as brown bears in Alaska, where they can grow *really* big with all that coastal seafood and salmon. What I find amazing, is that they can grow so huge and powerful by eating, in the main, berries. For a bear to eat thousands of berries a day it must be such a fiddle. It would drive me nuts if I had to gather berries to survive and I wouldn't need anywhere near as many and I've got dexterous fingers to help in the collecting. Of course, they can eat all sorts of other vegetation, carrion and fish and occasionally they do kill an animal themselves. Bears are all about eating. They are always on the lookout for food because they sleep for six months a year and on waking they have a short summer in which to build up their strength to survive the next six-month nap.

In Glacier Bay, Alaska we saw a lot of bears and they were huge. They were also unafraid of us. We were kayaking and could go quite close to a bear on shore who would see us but ignore us. It was a different situation here in the Yukon, where the bears ran for cover on seeing us. Perhaps Glacier Bay, being so remote hasn't had human hunters there and so the bears don't realize people can be such a threat. Why would they be if a person doesn't shoot at them, I mean, they are nine feet tall, have claws like machetes and teeth like daggers and have colossal strength.

Encounters with bears are a magical experience but we did have one hairy moment (excuse the pun) with a bear we didn't even see. We were in our tent, camped in Scidmore Bay, within Glacier Bay National Park. It was late at night and outside we heard a twig snap.

"Did you hear that?" I asked Gary, my guts twisting and my heart beginning to race.

"Yep."

There was then a loud snort from right outside the tent.

"Oh shit," breathed Gary. "Do you think we should have a look?"

"There's no way I'm sticking my head out the tent to have a bear knock it off," I said and with that I pulled my sleeping bag over my head like a child hiding from the bogeyman.

The seconds dragged by into minutes. There was no further sound.

"Do you think it's gone?" Gary asked.

"I dunno. I wish tents had windows."

"Yeah."

All we could do was lie there until we calmed down enough for us to be able to sleep. In the morning we discovered that it had indeed been a bear. Our food canisters had been scattered and a pan lid had been squashed, but the bear had got no food and so had left.

The water carried us onward and the spot where the curious bear had stood up to see us receded. The Yukon stayed narrow until midmorning when we passed 'Five-Mile Bend', at which point it opened out again. Five-Mile bend is named for its distance from Little Salmon Station, a small settlement on the confluence of the Yukon and Little Salmon Rivers. It is thought to be the oldest permanent First Nation Peoples' settlement on the upper Yukon. The village had originally been located on the opposite side of Little Salmon River, but it moved after a flu out-beak in 1917 which wiped out the original population.

Many of the cabins we passed at Little Salmon were very modern in appearance and looked as if they may be lived in all year. The cabins were serviced by the Robert Campbell Highway, which at this point, was still out of sight to us. Despite the settlement on the right-bank, the left still had the appearance of wilderness and just to prove how wild it was, another black bear wandered around on the shore. I thought how fine it must be to open your curtains on a morning and see a bear.

We drifted further on and a set of power lines came into view hugging the hillside, followed briefly by a glimpse of a juggernaut on the road. We passed between two islands in the river and the road was gone. On the shore of one of the islands was a huge driftwood tree, complete with root plate and most of its branches and next to it was yet another black bear. Ironically we were seeing more bears now, near the signs of humanity, than we had in the boonies.

A bend in the river took us away from the cabins and the road and we had lunch in a secluded spot at Mandanna Creek. The ground here was flat and the forest had the more open feel of managed woodland, which indeed it had been. Until the dearth of the paddle steamers there had been a wood camp here. The earth was springy with needles and several squirrels darted about on the ground collecting fallen cones, tails bobbing and bodies undulating sinuously as they ran. The silence was punctuated intermittently with the insistent yammer of them.

We tied the canoe to a tree and made ourselves comfortable amongst the trees sat on stools made of cut logs. The gas stove hissed frantically at the bottom of the pot, determined to ensure that the water inside it shared in its frenzy. While Gary checked out the map to confirm our location, I stared absently at the carcass of a moss-covered tree, which had fallen a long time ago. I wondered what creatures there were writhing about underneath its skin and within its body. Did woodlice live in the Yukon? I supposed they do. Perhaps they aren't as prevalent here as at home, because they don't like acid soil (they need calcium carbonate for their exoskeletons).

Interesting critters woodlice. There are about 32 different species which live wild in Britain alone (with about another 14 living in our greenhouses). They are thought to have evolved from benthic creatures that invaded the land directly from the sea without an intermediary phase in fresh water. Some of them, such as the sea slater still live on the beach onto which they had dared to emerge some 50million years ago. Still, they aren't as well adapted to life on land as other terrestrial arthropods as they don't have a water-resistant exoskeleton. They tend to be active at night and lurk under stones or in wood where it is damp. Underneath their body they have gills, which they must keep damp, sometimes dipping them in dew to soak up moisture.

Their staple diet is leaf litter and fungi, carrion and algae. They don't digest it too well first time around so they eat their own dung to process it a second time; nice. They have seven pairs of legs and sometimes in the summer if you turn one over you can see the females carrying their eggs in brood pouches filled with fluid alongside their legs. Depending on climate and species it takes from three months to two years to reach maturity and they grow in a series of moults. They are unique in moulting in two halves- the rear half is shed a few days before the head end, leaving at least one half of the body fully operational and tough whilst they go through this delicate transition.

My reverie over woodlice was broken by the sight of steam coming from the water pot and by Gary passing me a plate of cheese and crackers, the explorers ambrosia. A raven flew over and circled back, his tail a black diamond. I fancy he coveted my crackers.

As we left Mandanna creek after lunch the wind was starting to get up and as it passed through the treetops it sounded like a river rushing over a steep gravelly bed. Canoeing became hard work into the wind, despite the help of the current below us. The river had changed again and was wide, but strewn with islands, which seemed to funnel the wind into a shrieking banshee at some points. Of course, at those points where the wind seemed fiercest, it was never behind us.

Head down and working against the wind I felt like a galley slave. Instead of being driven by a whip it was my own determination to cover the mileage that forced me on. To keep moving it needed constant paddling and I dreaded being pushed back by the wind if I stopped for a rest or to turn around and talk to Gary. There comes a time, or at least there should, in an adventure holiday when you ask yourself, 'why am I doing this?' It's a time when you're tired, cold and miserable and only endurance and willpower will see you through. If you experience such a low it makes the pinnacles all the higher. How richly I value and appreciate a warm bed, a dry room and a hot meal, things that many people take for granted.

At two-thirty we landed on a sandy island in search of a respite from the wind. We seriously thought about camping there. I was desperate for a rest, but I didn't say any such thing to Gary. My shoulder was stiff and I pinwheeled my arm around to try and loosen it up. I had noticed last night that there was a huge bruise covering the whole of my left bicep. I thought that the muscle must have torn slightly and it had swollen up to a degree that would have taken weeks of work to achieve in the gym. It was a damn shame it would reduce to its original puny profile.

Despite my fervent desire for a rest there was little cover here from the wind and it was throwing the sandy soil against my ankles. The few pines that had managed to grow here were huddled on rough rocky ground and so shelter for the tent was not possible. There was also no suitable spot in which to cook that wasn't exposed to the gale. These factors, combined with the fact that it was so early in the day led us to feel that we should push on a little further to reduce the distance we would need to travel on our final day on the river.

After a short rest huddling from the wind as best we could behind the bole of a tree, with some reluctance, we headed back out onto the water. As the canoe slid once more into the Yukon I thought for a fleeting second how good it would be to have two of us paddling. I instantly felt a twinge of guilt because I hadn't asked how Gary was feeling for some time. I had been lost within my own world enjoying the river and whilst Gary's injury didn't impact on me I hadn't really been too concerned with it. I tried to justify myself by thinking that there was nothing I could actually do about his arm anyway.

As it turned out Gary had not been too concerned with the discomfort of his arm. By now it had eased to the point where it wasn't an issue until he tried to do something strenuous. What had been occupying his mind were feelings of guilt that I was battling this wind on my own whilst he sat there helpless through what he saw as his own stupidity. However, I didn't know that. I had only asked for Gary's thoughts when I had been writing this book and had come to point where I was struggling with writer's block.

I think the whole experience of our trip, followed by writing about it has highlighted to me my biggest fault, my selfishness. After Gary's accident and my relief at finding that he wasn't crippled, my next thoughts had been about how a lack of photographs would impact on my plans to write an article. Then I had been worried about not getting to see the Dempster Highway. And now I was thinking that I wished that there were two of us paddling in order to make my life easier. What a selfish bastard I am. Anyway, there was nothing to be achieved from dwelling on it, so I gritted my teeth and paddled on.

On our right, hidden by a huge island, lay Columbia Slough. This had been the site of one of the Yukon's biggest disasters. In September 1906 a steamer known as Columbia was heading downstream laden with three tons of blasting powder (sounds interesting already) several head of cattle and a 25-man crew. Amongst the aforementioned crew, was a boy called Phil Murray who owned a repeating rifle and took delight in taking pot shots at ducks whenever the boat pulled ashore.

In the slough a huge collection of ducks had gathered and Phil got so excited at the scale of the target that he forgot the rules which forbade shooting from the vessel. He grabbed the gun, but before he got chance to fire, Morgan, the fireman, took the gun off him and shouldered it to have a crack himself. As Morgan hurried to the ship's rail to get a good position he tripped and fired a round into a barrel of blasting powder. The result was cataclysmic. Six men, including Phil lost their lives but the Captain managed to ground the ship so that the rest of the crew could escape to shore.

Whilst on an Alaska State Ferry on the way down the Inside Passage I had read in a magazine that had been left in one of the lounges an amusing story about another hunter. It involved a man who was out on a lake in a rowboat fishing, and in all probability drinking, as this tale has all the hallmarks of a drink related incident. He hooked something big and for several minutes battled with a monster from the deep. With a final heave he hauled his catch into the boat, only to find himself face to face with a pissed off beaver. Armed with the tools of his trade, the beaver set about destroying the wooden boat and alarmed at the thrashing demon that was obliterating his vessel, the fisherman grabbed his gun. This was no doubt an elephant gun. He took careful aim and blew a substantial hole through the beaver and collaterally, through the bottom of the boat. The fisherman thus went down with his ship.

Just beyond Columbia Slough we finally found a suitable campsite on the inside of Mooreside Bend. The wind was still blowing and there were intermittent bursts of heavy rain, tempered with spells of drizzle. The sky glowered at us, prematurely dark and immensely threatening. I half expected an ear splitting crack of thunder. The sand at the water's fringe stuck to my boots and my footprints looked as if they were cast for time immemorial, not in sand, but in cement. I kept my eye open for other prints as I staggered about the rocks with my share of the barrels of food, bags, rucksacks, tent etc. but I didn't see any.

There was an open glade amongst the trees, which was obviously a well-used spot for people like ourselves. We sheltered under the pines and selected beanfeast and mash for our evening meal. In a sudden downpour we started to heat up the beanfeast on our one gas stove, the first time we had resorted to using it for anything other than a quick brew. Just as we got started the rain eased back to drizzle and I lit a fire using the husks of pinecones that a squirrel had left in a dry pile underneath a log. With the fire going in short order I heated the water for the powdered mash whilst Gary finished heating the beanfeast on the stove. More as a result of good luck than good management the different parts of the meal came together at the right time and we shovelled it in before the hard rain came back.

After our meal we squatted against the trunk of a big pine. There was an eighteen-inch circle around the tree, which was remaining totally dry. Beyond that, the fallen needles on the ground were twitching as raindrops hit them. With my back leaning on the trunk and my legs folded beneath me I watched the needles' dance. Unfortunately, it wasn't entertaining enough to overwhelm the cramp building in my legs and I had to stand up.

A squirrel dashed over to its pile of cones that I had disturbed. It chirred on noticing the disturbance and then ran off to collect some more. It was back at the double with the first of the replacements. I stood still, watching its labours as the rain pattered against my hat.

We could have put the tarp up for a shelter and sat underneath it to read, but then we would just have been sitting still and getting cold, so as the drizzle intensified we retired to the tent at 6.45pm.

Ensconced in my sleeping bag and envisioning our arrival in Carmacks and then Dawson the next day, I re-read the section in one of our guidebooks on the history of the Klondike Goldrush. In 1896 a mining prospector, Robert Henderson, panned a tributary of the Klondike and came up with 20-30cents worth of gold. He had been working in the area for two years following a tip from a man named Joe Ladue, a trader from the settlement of Ogilvie. Twenty to thirty cents was four times what he normally expected to come up with for a single pan. He worked that 'Gold Bottom Creek' all summer and one day when returning from Ogilvie on a re-supply trip, he bumped into another prospector, George Washington Carmack. Carmack was out fishing with his two First Nation brothers-in-law, Dawson Charlie and Skookum Jim, in the mouth of what would later be called the Klondike River. Following the prospectors' code, under which miners shared their finds as pickings were usually slim and the help of others was often vital, Henderson told Carmack of his find.

On 17th August 1896 Carmack panned Rabbit Creek and came up with $3-4 worth of gold a pan. The three of them staked claims on what would become known as Bonanza Creek and headed into Fortymile. On seeing his nuggets the inhabitants of Fortymile deserted town to stake their claims. In the days that followed Joe Ladue left Ogilvie to stake his claim and as he went he had the foresight to open a sawmill in a swampy area where the Klondike and the Yukon met. This would become Dawson City.

The story of the gold discovery is slightly different as told by the family descendants of the two First Nation men. Skookum Jim had once saved a frog that was trapped in a hole and in repayment for his kindness a frog-woman came to him on two occasions in his life, firstly to offer him a gift of food and the second time to offer him wealth.

Skookum Jim and Dawson Charlie (or Tagish Charlie, as I've read in some versions) went prospecting for several years and ended up in the Klondike region. They ran into Skookum Jim's sister and her husband George Carmack. They went hunting for moose to provide meat for the winter and after shooting one Skookum Jim went to a creek to get water for tea. In the creek he saw some heavy yellow rocks and took them to George Carmack to ask if these were the type of rocks that he was looking for. Indeed they were. The creek would become Bonanza and Skookum Jim would receive his gift of wealth from the frog-woman.

Whichever version you go for, by autumn that year the news had reached Juneau, by which time most of the best claims had been staked. Robert Henderson, still working 'Gold Bottom Creek' was unaware of the furore and by the time he did it was too late. The next summer when several prospectors arrived in San Francisco and Seattle with so much gold they couldn't carry it, America went insane in the rush for the Yukon. As the stampede began in late summer of 1897 many people already in Dawson left in a panic fearing that food supplies would not last the winter. A human tidal wave of 100,000 or more was sweeping north. Only the strongest 30,000 or so actually made it over the brutal Chilkoot and White passes that winter. Many of the rest simply gave up and turned back or died of scurvy, or froze to death, or committed suicide, or were murdered. Those 30,000 souls who did cross the mountains waited on the shores of the lakes that were the source of the Yukon and built a variety of craft to take them to Whitehorse via the Whitehorse rapids and then the last 460miles to Dawson.

The summer of 1898 saw the stampeders arrive in the Klondike, but by then every claim worth staking within 150km had already been staked. Those that had money established saloons and dance halls and casinos to plunder the wealth of the prospectors who had nothing else to spend their money on. For a year Dawson was a boomtown and then as quickly as it had sprang up it receded as news of a gold strike in Nome hit the headlines.

Chapter Eight

It was still raining, though only just, when we finally dragged our asses out of bed. I tried to squeeze my way out of the tent without touching the wet fly sheet with my shoulders or bare legs. As I stood up and loped over to the storage barrels with my laces flapping, a squirrel watched me with amused curiosity. I watched him back. He was sitting on a log shredding pinecones with a speed and dexterity that was really something to see. We kept an eye on each other as I tried to get into my trousers without letting the legs fall into the sandy soil, which was clingy with rain.

"Brew? On the burner?" Gary asked from behind me.

"Sounds good," I said, rummaging in the food barrel for our cereal bars. "I'll scoff this and then sort out the tent."

Whilst the stove heated the water we crammed sleeping bags into their stuff-sacks, folded and rolled our Therma Rests (Therma Rests are a type of bed roll which insulates your sleeping bag from the ground and smoothes out the bumps. I used to use a foam mat, but Therma Rests roll up much smaller and are self inflating when you open them out) and packed away the clothes we had slept in. The trees were tight around the tent, hanging down and trying to snag us as we went past. I tried not to touch them because doing so caused a cascade of rainwater. As we busied ourselves like ants over a picnic a small flock of chickadees appeared in a spruce. They are small birds, very much like great tits at home. They had strong flashes of white across their cheeks and they flitted around the tree like jerky clockwork toys.

I had noticed a distinct lack of passerine birds whilst we had been in the Yukon. We had seen ravens and eagles, kingfishers, harriers and mergansers, but no small songbirds. There had been no dawn chorus to welcome our day and by and large the woods were silent. Part of this is due to the nature of coniferous forest. There are fewer niches available, as the majority of the forest's foliage is concentrated very high up, unlike deciduous trees, which have leafy branches all the way to the ground. The coniferous canopy is so dense that little light reaches the floor and there is often a lack of understorey. Deciduous forest tends to have a wider range of tree species and there are shrubs, bushes and herbs on the ground. Deciduous trees themselves support a wider range of invertebrates. All this means that there are fewer opportunities for birds in a coniferous woodland. Of course, it was nearing winter and so many of the songbirds may have flown south. Perhaps though, there aren't many songbirds in the Yukon because the weather and other conditions are too harsh to permit the joviality of singing. I was hugely enjoying being in the Yukon's forests, there is nothing like walking around knowing that you might run into a bear or a moose, but there is a lot to be said for the gaiety of an English wood.

At home, the first members of the dawn chorus get started before the sun is anywhere near breaching the horizon. Robins, blackbirds and thrushes kick things off. They sing to attract mates, declare territorial boundaries and deter intruders. It's the time of day to do it. There is light to see by, good enough to spot predators, but it is sub-optimal for catching food such as small insects and so the time is better spent making one's self known. Any bird trying to feed will make a less profitable use of its time and so all the birds sing together as the sun comes up. The symphony can be spectacular. As the morning wears on, the singing subsides as feeding and preening take precedence.

The dawn chorus lasts on into the winter, albeit with far fewer members as the warblers have left for winter sun. Only when it's a really cold morning when frost or snow lies on the ground does the dawn finally emerge in near silence. On these mornings the birds have used up all their energy just surviving the night.

The chickadees moved off and the dexterous squirrel chirred piercingly in lieu of a bird and bounded off as I folded up the tent. As I brought it down to the beach for loading, Gary handed me a cup of tea. I stood on the shore and watched a gentle rain begin to fall again. The moving current rapidly distorted the circles of impacting raindrops. It was a fairly miserable morning. The rain got heavier, drumming on the brim of my hat and making the river sigh an extended hiss. On the far shore the rain blew in swirling curtains of misty vapour against the dark background of pines.

It was cold stood on the beach so I went and joined Gary squatting against the trunk of a huge pine. It was cold there as well, but it was dry. In fact, it was incredible how dry. The ground was still dust at the base of the trunk and yet it had rained overnight. I looked up into the dense swirl of needle-clothed branches above, through which there was no sign of the sky. As I finished my tea I watched once again as the rain caused fallen pine needles to jump outside the radius of protection offered by the tree. I enjoyed watching the rainfall that morning although I was hoping for it to stop before we got too far on the river. It's not often that I appreciate rain as it's usually cold and uncomfortable, but this morning I had recognized the beauty in its patterns and I appreciated that without it there would be little life here. It was rain and the resulting rivers that had, to a large degree, shaped the very landscape I was in.

This was to be our last day canoeing on the Yukon and I might have felt a little melancholy, but the presence of the rain made it easier to leave. Besides, I was excited about the prospect of the drive up the Dempster Highway. Even though we had been a bit later than usual in rising we had wasted no time packing up in the miserable weather and we were on the water by 8.10am.

Thankfully there was no wind and the incessant drizzle fell straight down and was fended away from my glasses by the wide brim of my Australian bush hat. The landscape was sullen in the grey light. In the constant drizzle and amid the huge expanse of the swelling Yukon there was not much to see and we landed at the 'Coalmine Campsite' in Carmacks at 10am without incident.

There was almost an incident at the campsite before we had even disembarked. We had become used to finding gravelly beaches to land on, but there were none of these at 'Coalmine'. The landing point was a wooden deck at the bottom of a steep bank. As we pulled alongside and I stood up to get out onto the decking, the canoe wobbled alarmingly and I nearly went into the drink. Hauling the gear up, and subsequently the canoe, was a slippery and onerous task.

Finally we were freed from the river and as I stretched my legs and back I took a moment to look at the river. It swirled silently onward, pushing rapidly towards Dawson, where we would meet it once more.

We left the canoe, paddles, life preservers and barrels for Kanoe People to pick up as arranged and then under the shelter of a big canvas marquee we packed the rest of our stuff into our rucksacks.

After availing ourselves of the campsite's shower we made plans to hike into town. However, for the princely sum of three bucks each, a lady at the campsite offered us a ride in her pickup. I got a free tongue in the ear from the German shepherd dog on the back seat, who seemed pleased about this unexpected journey as the heating was now on in his bedroom.

With time to waste before the arrival of the bus, we spent two-and-a-half hours in the Gold Panner restaurant eating burgers and apple pie and quaffing the odd tea and hot chocolate. There seemed to be absolutely nothing else to do in Carmacks. It didn't appear to be even a one-horse town. I crossed the dirt lot between the restaurant and the hotel, a journey that required a dance around rain filled potholes. I phoned Mel to let her know we were still alive, despite all predictions to the contrary, but only managed to get her brother, Kevin, who had gone to our house to dog sit while she was out. We then sauntered off and loitered on the forecourt of the Shell gas station where the Dawson City Courier bus would pick us up for the trip to Dawson.

Later, as the bus climbed into the hills to the north of Carmacks we looked down onto the Yukon. I could scarcely believe that we had paddled on there on our last trip to Dawson. The river was now frighteningly immense. I could only guess at its size, but it looked to be a mile wide. I felt very small and as the rain pelted the windows of the bus I gladly settled into my seat over the heater.

It was early evening when we got into Dawson and we trudged along Front Street to the end of town where the ferry, the 'George Black' ran a free, twenty-four hour a day, service connecting the town to the Top of the World Highway. We stood on the metal decking of the ferry, the only passengers aboard, exposed to a bitingly cold wind. We watched the lights of town recede as the ferry powered its way across the river, which had shrunk again to a less intimidating size, but the current had lost none of its oomph. I was surprised at how well the ferry seemed to cope with the racing tide. The hills and woods surrounding the town were already dark as we stepped off the ferry into the gloom. There were no lights here, as there was no settlement on this side of the river. The Top of the world Highway was only a dirt road heading into Alaska and the hostel we were heading to had no electricity or piped water. After a five minute walk we checked in, dumped our stuff in our room and headed back into town and into the embrace of the bar in the Downtown Hotel where we enjoyed a delicious meal and a beer or two.

I couldn't put it off any longer. I had to get up for a pee. I slithered out of my sleeping bag on the bottom bunk in our room and blundered into some more clothes. I say some more, because I had worn a fair few in bed. I lurched outside onto the wooden decking and raced up a flight of stairs to the men's urinals. I sped past a thermometer, which read -6 Celsius.

After a blissful pee, I checked out the scenery on the way back. The cabins of the hostel were set amongst a woodland of aspen, birch and pine and the deciduous trees were a mix of old green fading to new yellow and gold. The decking was littered with a dazzling multitude of leaf carcasses. We were on a hillside and below me was the Yukon and on the opposite bank, Dawson. Dawson is nestled right at the foot of an 885m mountain called the 'Midnight Dome' and its tree covered slopes provide a perfect backdrop for the town, or I should say city, although there are only around 2,000 permanent residents. Unlike many North American cities Dawson doesn't sprawl, it doesn't need to and sandwiched between a mountain and two rivers there isn't much room to do so even if it wanted to. Eight avenues and ten main streets are about it. As it's roughly only a mile long and not much over a quarter of a mile wide, you could walk all over town in a morning. All the buildings are of timber construction, the roads are dirt and the sidewalks, where there are any, are wooden boardwalks. It is a city like no other.

Although the view was sensational, my bed was calling me back and the frosty air was pushing me there, so I retired until the disgracefully late hour of 8am. When we finally emerged we dashed down to the ferry and headed straight into Klondike Kate's Restaurant for a slap up breakfast. Eggs, sausages, bacon and hash browns. None of this cereal bar shit.

After breakfast we wandered around town. Most of the buildings have been well maintained or beautifully restored. The town was declared a National Historic Site in 1960 and Parks Canada maintains some of the buildings. Much of the money for restoration has come from the gambling income of Diamond Tooth Gertie's casino. A set of buildings on First Avenue looked particularly good. They were painted in bright pastel colours. There was Jimmy's Place, a pale blue/green next to Curly's Hair Shop, the sign of which was lime green, set off with a red-and-white barber's pole. The barber's was next to a sweet shop with a white top to the building and an aquamarine bottom. Next door to that was Klondike Cream and Candy in bright pink. Next, in blue with dark blue windows and doors was Dawson Gifts and Gold. Sourdough Joe's Restaurant painted green, completed a set, which looked especially good from a distance with the hills behind them. It was like walking around on the set of a Wild West cowboy movie, except that the horses have been replaced with huge cars and pickups, which prowl and rumble slowly around the streets. One sign on the sidewalk read 'Cowboy Parking Only. Violators will be castrated.'

Two neighbouring buildings in the centre of town are slumped at odd angles, their timbers dry and flaky, un-restored relics of the gold rush. The taller of the two has a spectacular false front and it lists so far over that one of its ground floor windows almost touches the floor. They have literally sunk into the ground because they were built on regular type foundations. Unfortunately, as the ground here consists of permafrost, the floor of a heated building laid directly onto the ground causes the permafrost to melt and the foundations to subside. The rest of the town's buildings are built up on chocks to keep the heat away from the ground.

After an exploration of most of the town we headed out to hike up the Midnight Dome, taking a very steep trail following some power lines up into the woods from the end of Queen Street. I was soon sweating in my fleece and it came off, along with my jumper, leaving me in a T-shirt. I was reminded of walking in the Swiss Alps with Gary and two other friends some years ago. We were walking the Alpine Pass Route, a 210-mile trail from Sargans to Montreux. We had to cross 16 passes and the trails up to each one of them were precipitous. We started off on the first day full of blood and thunder, thinking that we were fit as fleas and that we would race up the trails. We were knackered in short order. Fortunately, at the start of our second day we spoke to a Swiss lady and we told her about how hard we were finding the walking. She gave us some of the best advice I have ever had.

"Walk slowly," she said, "as if you are an old lady. Slow steps. If you do that you will be able to walk constantly and you won't need to rest and you can go all day."

She was right. If you walk slowly you get into a rhythm and you don't get breathless. Over a long haul the tortoises beat the hares by a long, long way.

On Midnight Dome it was a beautiful day with a blue sky splashed with the odd fluffy white cloud. On the lower slopes we passed through a dense forest of birch and aspen, their trunks white in the sun and their leaves ablaze with gold. The leaves fell like snow flurries in the wind.

Above the tree line the ground was frozen like iron and the air had the bite of the arctic. My jumper and fleece were back on, as was a body warmer, waterproof coat, gloves and a woolly hat. The view from the top was stupendous. Below us, to the south-west, on the flat floodplain of the river was Dawson, laid out in a grid. In front of it ran the grey/brown waters of the Yukon. At the south end of town the black water of the Klondike fanned out adjacent to Front Street and was swallowed in the Yukon, which had snaked away around islands and between hills, on its journey from the south and Whitehorse. In the opposite direction the Yukon, which now looked blue in the distance, threaded its way north-west into Alaska. To the north-east we could see the tops of the Ogilvie Mountains fading into the distant haze, some of them crowned with snow, the Arctic Circle beyond them. On the hills across the river, where our hostel was, we could see the Top of the World Highway switch-backing up and away.

    Despite the awesome view and the bright sun we were driven from the peak by the wailing wind and the sub-zero temperature. We fairly sprinted down a different trail, heading for the shelter of the trees. We stopped and watched a ptarmigan strutting around on the trail for five minutes or so and then plunged down a dusty track back into town. At 2.45pm we had a triple-decker and fries in Klondike Kate's. Entering Klondike Kate's yet again I was starting to feel like Norm who has his own barstool in the TV series 'Cheers'. Every time Norm enters the bar, 'Cheers', everyone in there shouts 'Norm!' in salutation. I could imagine walking into KK's and everyone saying, 'Bob!' After lunch I spent the rest of the afternoon reading a novel by the wood burning stove in the hostel's common room, whilst Gary hiked up along the Top of the World Highway a distance to get some photos of Dawson from a different angle. I just couldn't be arsed. I was working up the strength to hike back into town to visit the Downtown Hotel where I intended to replace some body fat and sink a few of the local beers. My favourite brew was Kokanee beer, which is named after a type of landlocked salmon.

The next morning just as I got up at 8am, there was a flurry of real snow to go along with the leaf blizzards. Perhaps a flurry is an exaggeration. Tiny flakes of snow fell straight down very slowly. There wasn't a breath of wind to disturb their free-fall. They were few in number and so gentle were they, that watching them was soporific. Where they landed on the boardwalk I examined them, tiny intricate matrices of white which slowly dissolved into a black stain of water. As I watched the snow falling several leaves detached themselves from the birch trees which were taking their cue from the snow and preparing for winter. The leaves danced downwards to form a golden underlay for winter's white carpet.

We sauntered into town and paid a visit to the cabin of the poet, Robert Service. Robert Service had been born in Lancashire in 1874 and educated in Glasgow. He emigrated to Halifax, Canada in 1894 and did several jobs including stints in mills, as a woodsman, and ploughing fields. After moving to Seattle and then California he found himself a bank teller in British Columbia. In 1904 he was transferred to Whitehorse.

He wrote his first Yukon poem, 'The Shooting Of Dan McGrew' in 1906 and he moved to Dawson in 1907. The town was already in a state of decline since the gold rush had ended, but by now Service was making a living from his writing. His other most famous works include 'The Spell of the Yukon' and 'The Cremation of Sam McGee.' He returned to Europe and ended up living in France and marrying a French woman. He was an ambulance driver during World War One, about which he wrote many other poems.

Service's cabin is right at the back of town on Eighth Avenue, nestled into the slope of the Midnight Dome and surrounded by woods. It is a captivating spot in the autumn with birch and aspen shimmering in the breeze. The lawn in front of the cabin slopes downhill and so the front door is approached by a flight of steps made of small logs while the roof is a living matt of sod with a pair of moose antlers on the apex above the door.

Reading Service's poetry you can tell that he loved the wild and vast nature of the Yukon. He indicates that many of the prospectors who came here looking for gold inadvertently fell in love with the land itself and their motivation for staying here changed.

I work in the countryside and one hundred years after Robert Service recognized such emotional ties to the landscape I feel that I have been removed from the land. It is only on a wilderness trip such as canoeing on the Teslin that I am re-immersed in 'real life'. As a countryside ranger I may work outside in the weather, but I can duck out of the really worst of it and at the end of the day I come home into a centrally heated house and I eat and rest in the warm and dry. To a large degree the vagaries of the weather are irrelevant. To really experience nature one has to live out in it, experiencing the joy or the misery of the elements and exposed to the hazards created by untamed wildlife, fast flowing water, loose soil on steep ground, thorny plants and all the other threats that the world can conjure up. Living out in the wild brings me personally alive and I think that many people in today's society could gain something from getting closer to nature, though I'm not naive enough to think that getting rained on in a forest is the universal panacea for troubled city dwellers.

Like it or not; ignore it or bury it; I think a connection to the natural world is an important part of our psyche. After all, we were once inextricably tied into the cycle of life. The very fabric of society once revolved around the planting and harvesting of crops and the birth of new livestock. But nowadays our food arrives in the supermarket regardless of weather or season.

I think many 'townies' are now so far removed from the natural world that they don't even see it when they do happen to stray into it, because as I suggest it is 'irrelevant' to them. Many is the time I have led a guided walk and whilst I talk or walk with a group I can see that they are simply not registering the birds flitting around in the hedges or trees beside us. They even fail to see a deer prancing in the next field until I point it out.

The reason they are missing the blindingly obvious is due to the way that our brains process and filter the information coming in from our eyes and interpret the world we inhabit. We only 'see' what is relevant to us. There was a famous experiment done by Dan Simmons and Christopher Chabris of Harvard University in which they asked volunteers to watch a recording of a basketball game and count the number of passes made by one team. Early in the match a man dressed in a gorilla suit walks slowly across the court and despite being in shot for 45 seconds around 40% of the volunteers failed to spot him. When they were asked to watch the game with no task to do, the gorilla was immediately spotted by everyone. This shows to me how important a person's mindset is for interpreting the world around them. Make the outdoors and wildlife irrelevant to someone and they will no longer even see it.

Whilst some wildlife just isn't seen, how much of it is seen as repugnant? How many people are repelled by things they don't understand? How many insects are thoughtlessly killed because they fluttered into a home where they are seen as a disease carrying invader instead of a fellow creature possessed of its own delicate beauty? At work I try to instill at least a sense of awareness of nature in children, even if I can't drum up a sense of wonder. It can be an amusing business sometimes. I once had a group of six-year-olds out one summer in a park and we sat under the benevolent shade of a sycamore. We were talking about food chains. I was building a food chain with child actors. One kid from the class was the sun. Next to her in the chain was a boy-cum-leaf. I asked the class what creature might eat a leaf. Hands went up and the chosen hand was attached to a child who answered, 'a snail.'

"Great," I said. "You come and stand here, next to the leaf and you can be a snail. Now can anybody think of a creature that might eat a snail?"

I thought they might struggle with this, as my first thought was a thrush and I suspected that getting a thrush from six-year-olds might take some prompting, but no, hands went up like mushrooms in the rain. I pointed at a small boy near the back.

"A Frenchman," he said, with some authority and undeniably correct.

To try to gain the attention of children and adults I sometimes use some of the techniques developed by Joseph Cornell. In the 1970's Cornell influenced the way many environmental educators taught natural history to young children with his book 'Sharing Nature With Children.' As a result of his work many environmental educators now try to make children aware of the nature around them using games and activities. As an example, a class of kids left to their own devices will march into a woodland talking and not paying any attention to what is going on around them. So I sit them down, each with a piece of card and a pencil. They make a cross in the centre to represent themselves and then they sit in silence. I tell them that I bet sitting in silence for five minutes is something that they can't do. As they sit I ask them to listen and for every sound they hear they should mark it on the card. The mark should indicate the direction of the sound in relation to them and relatively how far away it was. The mark should be a simple representation of the noise, for example a zigzag for the buzz of a bee, a musical note for the song of a bird etc. Doing this they suddenly realize that there is more in the woods than just themselves.

Just along the street from Robert Service's cabin, is that of Jack London, the author of 'The call of the Wild' and 'White Fang'. He had sailed up north from San Francisco in July 1897 as a twenty-one-year-old prospector. His cabin had actually been located 120km south of Dawson on the North Fork of Henderson Creek. Unfortunately, he came down with scurvy and on his recovery he left the Klondike penniless, but his time in the Yukon had provided him with the inspiration to write his books. His cabin was re-discovered in 1936 by two trappers and subsequently, two replicas of the cabin were made with the original logs, one in his hometown of Oakland and one here in Dawson.

After looking at the cabins of Service and London we went back into Klondike Kate's. "Bob!" the waitresses silently called. I sat in my usual seat and threw down a club sandwich as if it was the last chance to gain some calories before a winter of hibernation.

After that we went over to Minto Park. It was a Sunday and a bright, if cold, day and a group of locals were playing softball. It looked like fun. The teams were mixed sexes and there was a lot of friendly banter, Mickey-taking and encouragement. Though the pitching was done underarm it was still tough for many of the batters to hit. A new batter walked out and the field moved around, expecting a big hit. The pitcher checked their positions and then pitched. The white ball skidded through the air and the bat arced around and down from behind the batter's shoulder. It connected with the ball in a sweet, loud, crack! The batting team cheered as the ball soared skyward, but the batsman didn't move, he could see it curving out of bounds. It soared onwards until its flight was blocked by the side of a building. The wall reverberated with the sound of the impact, just beneath a window. I wished I had been invited to play, but we were content to watch, even though the temperature was not conducive to sitting around.

The following day we were up at 6.30am. The plan was to pick up a hire car and drive the Dempster Highway to the Arctic Circle. Construction of the Dempster Highway to link Dawson to Inuvik by the Arctic coast, was begun in 1959. At that time oil and gas exploration was booming and the town of Inuvik was itself under construction. As the debate over whether to build the road as an access to Canada's mineral wealth took place it was announced that oil had been discovered at the half way point of Eagle Plain. In order to explore the find it was now vital to get a road through and so in January 1959 construction began.

Construction was extremely difficult as the summer season is short and in winter, temperatures can plunge to -50 Celsius. Machinery froze or fell through ice into rivers. The road itself is gravel. It sits on a gravel bed 1.2-2.4 metres deep so that as the surface absorbs the summer sun, it is high enough so that the permafrost beneath doesn't melt and so cause subsidence.

The 'oil discovery' of Eagle Plain turned out to be a false alarm. Spiralling cost and arguments between the Yukon and federal governments kept the construction to a sluggish pace and in 1961, after only 72miles had been built, work ceased. The highway still had no official name, but opposition politicians had called it 'the road to remorses,' whilst the isolated construction workers had dubbed it 'the road to divorces.' When the work stopped altogether it was 'the road to nowhere.' There was no further progress until 1968 when America announced the discovery of oil and gas in Prudhoe Bay. The Canadian government feared that the Americans would exploit the resource without any consideration of Canada and felt the need to assert sovereignty over their share of the Arctic seafloor and to claim islands in the Arctic Ocean, which until then had been left unclaimed by any nation.

On 18th August 1979 the road was completed between Dawson and Arctic Red River. The road now goes on into Inuvik, a total length of 450miles. It was named the Dempster Highway after William John Duncan Dempster of the Royal Canadian Mounted Police. As a corporal in the service he was known as the Iron Man of the Trail for his dog sled journeys between Dawson and Fort McPhereson.

Dempster had come to the Yukon in 1898 during the gold rush and he personally patrolled a 475-mile route that he established in the depths of winter. He ran the route ten times in four years. In 1911 he set off from Dawson in terrible weather in search of a lost patrol, finding them only a few miles short of Ft. McPhereson where they had died of exposure.

Even though we would be camping along the highway we were reasonably confident that we weren't going to die of exposure, given that we were setting off in a four-wheel drive GMC Jimmy. We were really excited about going to the Arctic Circle with the possibility of seeing the northern lights, Dall sheep, mountain goats, moose, caribou, wolves, lynx, wolverine and bears.

At the juncture of the Dempster and Klondike Highways we filled up with gas at the Klondike River Lodge and service station and set out on an adventure. A road sign gave a hint that this was to be no ordinary drive as it announced, 'Next services 370km.' We decided to go straight to Eagle Plains and camp there overnight, cross the Arctic Circle the following day and then come back slowly, hiking and camping as we went.

There are not superlatives worthy of describing the scenery we passed over the next three days. Magnificent; awesome; majestic; stunning; breathtaking; beautiful and sublime are words that barely scratch the surface of what it means to be in such spectacular wilderness. I am privileged I have seen it and I was humbled by the experience. We set off up into the Ogilvie Mountains and up into Tombstone Territorial Park. At the south end of the park the dense, mixed, arboreal forest gave its best autumnal display with the snow-capped peaks and blue sky behind it.

As we climbed higher the trees thinned to be replaced by the odd patch or individual spruce. As the Tombstone Range appeared on our left we pulled into the North Fork Pass Overlook and looked along the valley of the North Klondike River. The trees were now largely gone and replaced with tundra and the broad sweep of the vast glaciated valley had been turned crimson by dwarf birch, splashed with the yellow of dwarf willow. The river was a silvered ribbon rushing in white horses over its rock-strewn bed, its race fuelled by melting snow. Tombstone Mountain itself, though standing at a drunken angle looked down from beyond the head of the valley, twenty-eight kilometres away, with a domineering permanence.

The Tombstone Range is formed from a type of granite known as syenite. Subduction of the ocean plate at the north-west Pacific coast created the volcanoes of the St Elias and Wrangell ranges and caused heating further inland where molten syenite rose to within a few kilometres of the surface. These blocks of igneous rock are known as plutons, or where large or numerous are called batholiths. The rock lying above the tombstone pluton had been a soft sedimentary rock, which had worn down extremely quickly leaving Tombstone jutting skyward.

On we travelled into the Blackstone Range and the crest of the continental divide at North Fork Pass Summit, the highest point on the highway at 4,229feet. To the north the land is drained by the Blackstone, Ogilvie, Peel and Mackenzie rivers, which head for the Beaufort Sea in the Arctic Ocean. Behind us, to the south, the North Klondike River drains into the Klondike river and then to the Yukon, which eventually spills into the North Pacific. Here the ground hugging vegetation had faded to brown and snow had already been falling, but only enough had lain to fill the gaps between the plants. The valley floors were a patchwork of white and brown and I was strongly reminded of the wintry Highlands of Scotland. The edges of the lakes and tarns were sheathed in ice, the remaining open water still as glass, and reflecting a perfect image of the white peaks in respectful homage.

From here on we would be travelling into a land that was once part of a sub continent known as Beringia. During the last two million years a succession of 'ice ages' has occurred with warmer spells in between big freezes. During the ice ages much of the Northern Hemisphere was under huge ice sheets. So much water was locked away in ice that the sea level fell by as much as 150metres, exposing a land bridge between Siberia and Alaska. This land bridge, eastern Siberia, much of Alaska and the northern part of Yukon Territory made up Beringia.

Due to the way the ice sheets formed and subsequently grew, they surrounded Beringia and as moisture-laden air travelled inland it dumped its precipitation over the ice sheets leaving Beringia in a rain, or snow shadow. Without accumulating snow, ice sheets never scoured the area and it became a steppe covered in hardy grasses. This sea of grass, which in warmer inter-glacial periods developed forests, became populated at various times with creatures such as mammoths, giant short-faced bear, scimitar cats, American lion, yesterday's camel, giant beaver and steppe bison.

The remains of these creatures have turned up as fossils and many of these have been found by prospectors. A lot of fossils were dug from the ground around Dawson during the gold rush. KoYukon people from the lower reaches of the Yukon River have recalled how the souls of the dead used to travel up the river to the place now occupied by Dawson. Here those souls would wait to be reborn and while they waited they hunted and fished as they had done in life. The animals they killed were called the 'underground game' and their bones could be found in the rocks.

15,000 years ago the last ice age began to recede, sea levels rose and central Beringia (the land bridge) was flooded. The grass steppes were gradually covered in forest as precipitation increased allowing tree growth and the grazing mammals such as mammoths, steppe bison and horses died out. Their loss was accompanied by the loss of their predators such as scimitar cats and lions. Before the land bridge was finally cut off by the rising tide a significant mammal species, *Homo sapiens*, managed to migrate from the old world to the new and their efficient collaborative hunting no doubt helped speed up the demise of the mammoth.

On cresting North Fork Pass the highway slipped down from the Blackstone Range following the Blackstone River. The trees returned and the gentler snowy hills became coated in a stubble of spruce. A red fox jinked between two boulders as we drove past. It was both familiar and at the same time, oddly alien, as I hadn't expected to see such a reminder of home.

At this point the limestone mountains have been weathered into gently rounded hills, but many ridges are composed of dolomite and they form towering columns known as tors. The jagged tors make some of the hills look like the backs of sleeping dragons.

At kilometre 102 (kilometre markers hug the roadside counting up the distance travelled from the Klondike Highway) we came upon Two Moose Lake and pulled over into the small car park. The lake gets its name as it is often used by moose to graze aquatic vegetation. We got out of the car and felt the wind race through our fleeces. I scanned the water with my binoculars in the hopes of seeing something, but alas, today there was no sign of any moose. The water's edge was crusty with ice and the middle of the lake looked strangely resistant to the wind, perhaps heavy with ice crystals that were growing in number, ready to seize the open water in a rapidly solidifying porridge. I looked at a booklet I had picked up in Dawson entitled, 'Yukon's Wildlife Viewing Guide' that built up my hopes of seeing American widgeon, gray cheeked thrush, American pipit, harlequin ducks, American coots and red-necked phalaropes. My hopes were dashed. The water seemed bereft of life.

I couldn't complain though as the view was something to marvel at and it wasn't as if we hadn't seen a moose before. We had seen several and one particular encounter sticks in my mind. We had been hiking in the Canadian Rockies on the Caribou section of the Great Divide Trail a few years previously. I remember walking uphill beside a stream in dense pine forest. It was mid-afternoon and it had been raining all day.

The stream beside us was pounding along its bed in a noisy, rain-fuelled rage, masking the sound of our trudging walk. We turned a corner and came face to face with a bull-moose. Now you might think moose are comical looking creatures, but I can assure you there is nothing comical about them when you are stood next to one. This was September, the time of the rut, when male moose have grown huge antlers with which to fight each other and they are chock full of testosterone and really, really touchy.

For what in reality was probably less than a second, but which seemed like minutes, humans looked at moose and moose looked at humans. The moose was dripping with rainwater and just looked pissed off. Its shoulders rippled with muscle and it looked as hard as granite. It was probably seven feet tall with antlers almost five feet across and it weighed something like half a ton.

Blood pounded in my ears, my legs froze and my life might have flashed before me if my brain had retained its capacity to function. The moose decided to make the first move, which thankfully was to turn and run into the stream. It bounded in and erupted out the other side with barely a break in stride and then looked back at us from behind a tree. With the immediate threat of death over, my brain function returned and I managed to photograph the moose before it disappeared.

At Two Moose Lake, we re-boarded the car and luxuriated in the break from the wind and the in-car heating. Fifty-two kilometres further on we crossed Windy Pass, leaving the Blackstone River behind and joined Engineer Creek, a tributary of Ogilvie River. The trees returned once more in a riot of colour and even the rivers were eager to contribute to the landscapes colour scheme; we followed a watercourse known as Red Creek for a short distance, its waters grey with silt. Several volcanic springs discharge into Red Creek and its water is high in dissolved calcium, magnesium, bicarbonate, sulphate, hydrogen sulphide, sodium and chlorine. The rocks of the creek bed were stained red with minerals, which stood out boldly in contrast to the surrounding snow.

At kilometre 259 we passed over Ogilvie Ridge and looked down into the Peel River valley. The aspen and birch had deserted us again and only dwarf spruce managed to maintain a toehold on the land. It was a forest in miniature as the tallest of them was little over five feet in height, dark green and dusted with snow. The gaps between the trees were filled with the reds and yellows typical of the tundra.

The sky was threatening with dark clouds promising more snow, yet from somewhere the sun peeked through a gap and the Peel River sparkled in the distance. Only forty kilometres shy of Eagle Plains hotel we came across a broken down car and two First Nation guys. We pulled over to see if we could help. The car seemingly needed a new battery and the attention of a mechanic, so we offered the two guys a lift to Eagle Plains, which is where they had set off from. I was nervous for the first few miles with these two strangers sat behind me. I kept worrying that the breakdown was staged to trap mugs like us, so we could be robbed. I think I've watched too much TV, most of it, the evening news.

As the kilometres clicked by, their passage recorded by the odometer, which I was watching, hoping to make it to Eagle Plains before we were brutally murdered, I began to relax. This far from civilization you are obliged to help people in trouble, because not doing so could get someone killed. Besides, I reasoned, why set up an elaborate car-jack when victims are so few and far between, in a place where the escape route is not exactly convoluted and suitable for throwing off pursuing police. Although the Dempster Highway isn't exactly a hotbed of crime the police do maintain a presence here. The Royal Canadian Mounted Police have a one tonne four-by-four crew cab truck upon which sits a camper. Members of 'M' division volunteer on a weekly basis to patrol the highway during the summer, which they do in their holiday time, often with their families. Each patrol is a six-day return journey from Dawson to Inuvik.

Behind us, after the initial 'where're you from? What you doing?' type conversation, the two breakdown victims became pretty quiet. Both of them were inscrutable behind dark sunglasses. I know from experience that breaking down is no fun, although I once did get a chuckle from such an incident.

I had been hitchhiking from Teesside to Liverpool in my cash strapped days as a student. If I remember rightly I was on my third ride and had got onto the M62. I'd been picked up by a guy in a Ford Sierra, or something similar, and only a few miles down the road the engine started to splutter. We managed to make it to the next junction, but the engine had finally died on the slip road. My chauffeur, fortunately, had breakdown cover and a mobile phone so I decided to wait with him. I could have tried thumbing it straight away, but reasoned that if the problem was fixable this dude was going right into Liverpool and so in the long run I'd be better off waiting here.

Much to my delight the RAC arrived within twenty minutes and the mechanic wasted no time in getting his head stuck underneath the bonnet. He tinkered, prodded and poked for a few minutes while the driver looked on with a worried expression.

"What do you reckon?" he finally asked, unable to wait any longer for some news. The RAC man looked up from the engine without standing up. He did that sucking-air-in-through-the-teeth thing that all mechanics do when they are about to tell you that you'll need to re-mortgage the house to pay their bill and then he said the immortal words,

"I reckon you're about fucked."

It was such a surprising thing for him to say that I laughed out loud. I couldn't help it. I was laughing all the way along the road and into the service station, where I got a lift within ten minutes. It was the one and only time I've been amused by anything relating to car mechanics.

Eagle Plain, when we finally got there alive, consisted of a gas station, a motel and a campsite, set in a blaze of crimson dwarf birch. We dropped off the two breakdown victims who were greeted by friends in the foyer of the motel. We left them doing elaborate handshakes and being offered beers to go and pitch our tent.

We found a small stand of spruce, which for some reason had grown in stature from the dwarf affairs we had seen along the highway and we pitched our tent amongst them. Not far beyond our tent the earth fell away off the plain and down to the Eagle River. The vista before us was immense.

With wood provided by the campsite we built a fire and prepared a meal of meatballs and boiled potatoes. Although the fire heated our food, any spare heat was whisked away by the wind and we shivered as we ate. I can recommend Eagle Plains campsite; the toilet block is probably the warmest on the planet. As I entered, the temperature lurched from sub-zero to sub-tropical. I took a shower just to prolong the time spent out of the cold.

The sunset that night was nothing short of spectacular, the sky and the clouds glowing radiantly blue, yellow and red above the regal silhouettes of the spruce. As the light faded and the cold intensified we headed into the hotel bar, our plan to drink beer slowly until it was late enough to look for the northern lights.

The bar had huge plate glass windows looking out over the remains of the sunset. We sat down in blissful warmth with a couple of cold Kokanee's. The bar was sparsely populated with us, a group of six truckers sat around a table and two lady tourists from Germany at the bar. The tourists were asking the barmaid if the road got any worse further on. They didn't have a four-wheel drive vehicle they explained and they had found getting this far a bit harrowing. There had been a few times during the afternoon when we had not exactly aquaplaned, but mudplaned over a gravely slurry and the road had become very rutted to the point when I considered the switch to four-wheel drive. The barmaid asked the advice of the truckers who unanimously declared that the road did get worse, but not much, and that they should make it to Inuvik. The prospect of a worsening road and the promise that they 'should' make it convinced the women to turn back in the morning!

The bar, being only 37km short of the Arctic Circle, had a suitable frontier feel to it. Spread out over one wall was a huge grizzly bear skin and close to that was a similarly-posed musk oxen. A stuffed arctic fox stalked amongst the spirits above the bar and a nicely posed wolverine lurked on a high ledge near the door. The mounted head of a Dall sheep looked out over the pool table and close to that was a moose head. The moose head was titanic. In life the animal's head and neck alone would have easily outweighed me.

There was an upright piano against one wall and above it was a mounted caribou head. The table football was presided over by a mountain goat and above the huge window lurked a musk ox head. The chandelier was composed of interlocked caribou antlers and other frontier paraphernalia on the walls included animal traps and snowshoes. In this day and age it wasn't terribly P.C to have so many stuffed and mounted animals, although I overheard the barmaid reassuring the German tourists that at least some of the animals were road-kill.

We finally slinked out of the bar at 11.30pm. The night was clear, with stars twinkling in a black sky, but as yet there was no sign of the northern lights. The frigid air throbbed to the gentle rhythm of a distant generator, but beyond that there was no other sound. Fortunately, with the temperature below zero, we didn't have far to walk 'home'. The tent was a mere hundred metres away. However, that was still distance enough to cause a well-known phenomenon, that of leaving a bar and then within five minutes needing the loo. I used to think this just happened to me, that I had some sort of intermittent bladder problem. But no, reassuringly it happens to others, more often when the walk home has no cover whatsoever and when entry back into the pub is not possible. There is a physiological explanation, which at least for me makes the phenomenon a bit more tolerable. Inside the pub it's warm and the capillaries in your skin open to let your blood dump heat. As you walk outside the temperature falls sharply and your capillaries close to conserve heat. This pushes blood into the core of your body and as a result your blood pressure rises. In order to lower the pressure your kidneys are spurred into draining fluid and so part way down the road you need a pee.

I had to go back to the toilet block to clean my teeth anyway, so tonight my bladder wasn't too much of a problem. It was way too cold to hang around watching the sky and so we retired to the tent and our sleeping bags. (Apparently, according to my friends, I may be soft. The temperature was not far below zero degrees Celsius, which is too cold a temperature for me to hang around at, but perhaps the likes of Sir Ranulph Fiennes and Chris Bonnington would break out their swimming trunks at such temperatures). By 3am. the diuretic properties of alcohol were in evidence and Gary got up for a pee.

"Bob, you'll have to get up, the Northern Lights are on," he said from amongst the spruce.

I pulled on my fleece and boots and joined him outside, where a huge proportion of the heavens was illuminated by a ghostly light. From just above the trees a green cloud seemed to blow southwards, lifting up like a dust devil in the wind. A bright moon shone next to the billowing display and the stars managed to glitter through it. It shifted in waves and sudden jumps and the colour faded to white.

The northern and southern lights occur as a stream of charged particles from the sun (the solar wind) hit the atmosphere. At high latitudes the earth's magnetic field funnels the particles into the ionosphere. Around one hundred kilometres above the ground the particles collide with atoms and molecules in the atmosphere, boosting their electrons' energy levels. To return to their normal state the electrons lose energy by emitting light. Oxygen molecules glow red, oxygen atoms glow green and nitrogen glows blue.

To take photographs of the aurora we had to set up tripods and had to shift from spot to spot as the display snaked its way around the sky. We fiddled with exposure times and aperture settings and made educated guesses as to what would work. I did all this dressed in my long johns with my bootlaces flapping, as I hadn't had time to tie them. I was too busy moving the camera or holding the shutter open to dress properly, keen to get shots before the show was over. I couldn't operate the camera adequately with gloves on and my fingers were screaming in protest at the cold, as was my ass. How I suffered for my art.

After half an hour the northern lights had begun to fade and I gratefully crawled back into my sleeping bag.

Chapter Nine

The light on my eyelids woke me up just before 7am. It was strange. I was camping in the Yukon Territory, but I could hear something other than the wind, a river or an animal. As my consciousness rose I realized it was a truck engine. I staggered out of the tent and crossed over the gravel parking lot for a vital visit to the planet's warmest toilet block.

Eager to set of on the final 37km to the Arctic Circle we had a hasty cereal bar breakfast with a cup of tea and set off. The road plunged down from the escarpment and crossed Eagle River. Gradually areas of black spruce muskeg were replaced by open tundra, but it was not boring to look at. The ground cover of bearberry, kinnikinnick and huckleberry had turned scarlet and some dwarf willow added its yellow to the canvas. Between these two bright colours were empty areas of gravel to complete a mosaic which often seemed to be laid out in roughly hexagonal patches. Beyond the tundra to the front and right lay the Richardson Mountains, their flanks brown in the haze and their peaks white with snow. With the slight changes in topography enhancing the effect, the road snaked away from us and remained visible in the dips and swells of the landscape for miles as a bright ribbon.

At the sign that marked the Arctic Circle at latitude 66 degrees, 33minutes north I pulled over. From this point onwards the mid-summer sun doesn't go below the horizon and the further north you go the more days there are of permanent sun. Of course the flip side of this is that at the mid-winter solstice the sun doesn't come above the horizon.

We set up our tripods and photographed ourselves by the signpost in suitably intrepid explorer-like poses. We also photographed the view. I had imagined that at this point there would just be flat boring desolation, the line of the Arctic Circle being no different from any other patch of tundra. However, beyond the interpretation sign the land fell away before us to a small creek, populated with a few black spruce. The ground cover had turned the ground to flame and the white tipped Richardson Mountains looked down kindly on us. It was a scene worthy of a photograph on its own merit and not just because it represented a line of latitude that was steeped in the history of human endeavour.

We drove on another 3-kilometres just to make sure that we were well into the arctic and then headed back. It was late morning when we got back to Eagle Plains for a toilet stop and a muffin. It was then off into the trusty Jimmy and the ride back to the Blackstone Ranges. We had just rejoined the forest in the run up to the Ogilvie River road-bridge when we turned a corner and there was a wolf. It had just been about to set foot on the highway to cross when we appeared and it turned tail and bolted. It bounded over three patches of dwarf willow that partially obscured its escape route, its tail a bouncing brush and then it was gone amongst the trees. We had had sight of it for all of four seconds at most, but that was enough to make an indelible memory. It had been a huge animal, its coat a shaggy white mass of fur. I was amazed at its size. In stature it was a similar height to a Great Dane, but it was longer and much bulkier looking. I swear I could have thrown a saddle over it and ridden it.

When I returned from the Yukon I couldn't stop thinking about how large the wolf had been. I couldn't get over it and I wondered, 'how big do wolves actually get?' I turned to a book I have at home, 'The Way Of The Wolf', by L. David Mech. Mech has studied wolves for forty years and is a world renowned expert. In 'The Way Of The Wolf' he says that the largest wolves inhabit mid-latitude Canada, Alaska and the old Soviet Union, where they can weigh as much as 175 pounds (twelve and a half stone). There are even reports of a wolf from the Yukon area that supposedly weighed a whopping 227 pounds! (That's over sixteen stone). I'll never know how big our wolf actually was, but I'm absolutely sure that it weighed substantially more than my 140 pounds.

Slowly, I drove the car the last few hundred yards to the bridge and walked out over the water in the hopes that the wolf would emerge from the trees and cross the river. The view from the bridge was beautiful. The river was crystal clear and rushed below us with a gentle whisper. Gravel beds broke the surface in tan patches of pebbles and others lurked below the surface in cold grey mounds like the backs of cruising sharks. The sky was blue and the mixed forest around us was dark green and yellow. I soaked up the sun and willed the wolf to come into view. In my mind's eye it trotted through the river flinging diamonds of water ahead of it, its coat astonishingly white against the dark blue of the water. It wasn't to be. Of the wolf there was no sign.

This hadn't been my first sighting of a wolf though. We had been lucky enough to see one in Glacier Bay.

We had been camped in Scidmore Bay, the same place where the brown bear would later scare the crap out of us while we lay in our sleeping bags. We had camped in that spot for two nights and after the first, bear-free, night we had walked along the shoreline in search of fresh water. I was walking in my hiking boots as my left heel had a blister from walking about in my wellies. Wellingtons were de rigeur for getting in and out of the kayak and they were good in the almost constant rain, but that morning my feet had protested and I had gone back to hiking boots.

The sky had been heavy and threatening rain and the snowy mountain above us, which late the day before had looked startlingly beautiful in the sunshine, now glowered darkly, promising to hurl a storm at us. We walked along the beach, the sea to our left and a thicket of Sitka alder, willows and cottonwoods to our right. After roughly a mile we came across an out-wash fan pouring a shallow glacial stream of water into the bay. I squatted down to filter drinking water into our five-litre water bladder. I was half-way through when Gary, stood just behind me, said very quietly and deliberately,

"Bob, there's a wolf."

I stood up so fast that my head almost reached escape velocity. I looked this way and that, desperately trying to see the wolf before it disappeared. And there it was, moving away from me towards the bay. It loped over the ground effortlessly and in a second its bouncing strides had taken it over the crest of the berm.

I dropped the filter and without a word we set off in the direction the wolf had headed. We jogged through the stream in a crouch, hidden from the beach by the crest of the berm. Icy water poured in over the top of my hiking boots.

"Shite!" I cursed in a hoarse whisper.

In a crouch we scrambled up out of the valley that the stream had carved in the gravelly beach. We peeked our heads up above the crest and were rewarded by sight of the wolf down near the tide-line. It turned and started to lope back up the beach in our direction. Its back and sides were black, but its muzzle was grey. Grey fur covered its thighs but its lower legs were black. Between its rolling shoulder blades was a dense patch of white, which looked as if it was being lost in the spring moult.

We stood stock-still and held our breaths as the wolf trotted up the beach. It moved with a fluid grace, its shoulders rolling slightly and its ankles seeming to repel it from the ground as its pads touched the stones. On it came. It had seen us by now and as it moved on it watched us closely, its head swivelling to keep us in sight though its body never veered from its course. It looked quite small, hardly any bigger than my German shepherd dog and I suspected that it was a female. As if to confirm my thought, she squatted briefly to pee. The wolf passed within 60-metres of us. I could never have dared hope to see a wolf in the wild. Only in my wildest dreams had I seen one so close. I was thrilled, a lifetime ambition fulfilled.

With my attention focused on the wolf I hadn't really appreciated the true beauty of the scene of which we were a part, until I got home and looked at our photographs. Beyond the wolf the bay, despite the drizzle, which had begun to fall, was a silver mirror in which sat a spruce-coated island. Behind the island were blue-grey mountains with snow capped peaks under a leaden sky. The wolf within the scene was the epitome of beauty and the essence of true wilderness.

On the Ogilvie River road bridge I couldn't help but feel slightly disappointed that we didn't see the white wolf cross the river, so I chided myself for being greedy. We had parked the car in a gravel pit at the southern end of the bridge and we went back to it to get our water bottles, daypacks and spare clothes for a hike up nearby Sapper Hill.

The hill was named after the army engineers who had built the highway. Its ridges and crest were littered with tall grey columns and mounds of monolithic dolomite. We set off slowly up the steep trail through the white spruce of the lower slopes. We clapped and called sporadically to scare away bears and in the bright sun I started to overheat.

"Hold on a sec. Gaz, I'll have to take some gear off. I'm sweating like a glass blower's arse."

Stripped off down to T-shirts we reached our first tor perhaps three quarters of the way up. It was made of several vertical sections fused together like the trunks of titanic trees fighting for space. As soon as we stopped walking we could feel the breeze which raced through our clothes. There was little warmth now in the sun and the vegetation was turning distinctly alpine.

Looking out to our right as we faced uphill we could see the Blackstone Range of mountains, their profiles rounded down to humps by erosion. The hillsides were stubbled with spruce and white with snow. This seemed odd as we were at a greater altitude and yet there was no snow here. Perhaps this hill had been just beyond the weather front that had dumped snow on the hills nearby, after all I reasoned, the edge of a front had to be somewhere. I remember being at home at about fifteen years of age. I was in the lounge and it started to rain heavily in the front garden. Some instinct made me leap up and run to the back of the house and look into the back garden where for several seconds there was no sign of rain. Then the front moved over the house and the back too, was engulfed in the shower.

I didn't ponder too deeply at these meteorological oddities as instead I turned to my left and looked down on the river in the hopes of seeing our wolf. I scanned the forest with my binoculars but saw nothing move.

Onwards and upwards. At the top of the hill where the soil petered out against the walls of the summit tor we climbed a ridge in the rock-face. From a tiny crack in the surrounding rock we took it in turns to look out over the view. It was awesome. We had gained 1100 feet in elevation and below us the river snaked through a flat valley floor bronzed by the autumn. The road was a thread following the base of the hills and we could just make out a tiny cabin. Who lived there? Did they live here through the winter? We would never know. Feeling a bit giddy from our eagle's perch we began the descent to the car.

Only a kilometre further down the road we pulled into Engineer Creek Campground at 6.15pm. A very short road led into the trees and fifteen short spurs led off it to individual pitches big enough to fit an RV (recreational vehicle, i.e. a camper van) and a tent. At each tent or trailer pitch there was a metal enclosed fire-pit and a picnic table. At the far end of the campsite road there was a small shelter and some long-drop toilets. Water was available in the creek.

We picked our pitch on the basis that the sun was shining full on the picnic table. The table was a luxury that we used to write our diaries on and to air out our sleeping bags over. Although there was a stack of firewood available by the shelter it was in large pieces and without an axe or saw we couldn't make use of it. The branches we found amongst the trees were wet and rather than wasting too much time struggling with a reluctant fire, we broke out the stove for our meal.

As the sun faded in the early evening a ghostly moon appeared above the cliffs that raced up from the far bank of the creek. We could see the stark edge of the cliff above the trees from our tent and the rock seemed to glow with a faint blue in the fading light. The temperature began to plummet and by the time we had eaten our evening meal we could stand it no longer and retired to the welcoming embrace of our sleeping bags. Gary set the alarm on his watch for midnight and at twelve fifteen he got up to check for the northern lights.

"Bob you have got to see this," he announced as I tightened my bag against the chill of his exit.

"I can't be arsed," I said.

"No honestly you have to get up. This is amazing."

I could hear him rummaging through his bags and I recognized the familiar clicking of a tripod being assembled.

"It's too cold," I protested, content that the photos I had of the northern lights from Eagle Plains would do just fine.

"Just stick your head out of the tent at least."

"Bloody hell. Alright then," I capitulated and wriggled forward just enough so that I could stick my head out without exposing too much flesh to the air.

"Jesus Christ!" I exhaled.

"Told you."

The sky was awesome. It was black velvet, studded with stars and low down, casting the tops of the trees in silhouette, was a thick band of green and white light stretching right across the dome of the heavens. I got up as the whole display waved and swirled. I scrabbled for my camera gear and was back to poncing about in long johns, my fingers turning to sausages and my backside being bitten by the frost. But it was worth it. Huge areas of the sky were covered in light and at one point an immense waving ribbon of green was topped in white with an underscore of bright red. It was a truly stunning display. It was captivating, but also slightly unnerving in a way I can't quite put my finger on. After maybe three-quarters of an hour the best of it seemed to be over. Back in my sleeping bag with pins and needles irritating my hands and feet as the blood returned I said to Gary,

"Thanks for making me get up."

"No problem," he said.

We got up at 7.30am. It was bitterly, bitterly cold. So cold that we didn't want to eat breakfast. We raced about packing up our gear and we just threw the tent, sleeping bags, Therma Rests and other crap into the back of the car loose. When the engine started the digital display above the rear view mirror showed the air temperature to be –6 degrees Celsius.

The car crunched over the gravel and out of Engineer Creek onto the highway as the snowy hills ahead of us blushed pink in the dawn. A few kilometres down the road when the engine had warmed the car we ate a cereal bar breakfast and then enjoyed the scenery heading up to the Blackstone Uplands. The sky was a perfect deep blue and laid out before us the mountains were huge, silky piles of icing sugar.

By mid morning we found ourselves back in the pullout that looked down the valley of the North Klondike, headed by Tombstone Mountain. Outside the confines of our metal cocoon the pair of us soaked up the view and the cold air. Although it was only two days since we had last been here the intensity of the colour in the vegetation had faded a little. The best of the autumn display would last, at best, two weeks at this latitude.

Gary took the gas stove out and sheltering as best as he could behind the car he brewed up. The wind was thick with fluffy fireweed seeds racing to who-knew-where, their fate dependent entirely on luck. There have been times when I've felt like a fireweed seed, racing through life on an ornery wind, chance encounters enhancing or detracting from the ride. I probably wouldn't have been squatting behind a car in one of the most beautiful parts of the world if I hadn't met Gary. I could not have blundered into a better, more adventurous travelling companion.

I certainly could not have collided with a more remarkable woman. Melanie indulges my yearning for wilderness with a forebearance that not many women could muster. When I think of how lucky we were to have met I think of a Tom Petty song, 'A Face in the Crowd', from the album 'Full Moon Fever'. The gist of which is that before we met and Mel became precious to me, she was just a face in the crowd; an unknown future, filled with chance encounters is what life is all about. I've enjoyed the ride so far and I seem to have fallen, at least temporarily, on fertile ground.

The water boiled and we fortified ourselves with tea before an assault up the side of Goldensides Mountain. This would be a two-thousand-foot climb. The landscape was open and treeless and the trail started with winding paths leading through the low shrubbery. The paths all led to the bottom of a steep slope broken and cratered with talus and scree. From the bottom looking up it was daunting. This would be a very steep ascent going up beyond the snow line. There seemed to be no path. It was a case of find your own way up the scree slope between two sharp ridges. Slowly, slowly, as we had been taught in Switzerland, we began the climb.

Up ahead I could see two people. A woman furthest up, followed by a man, fifty metres back. I kept glancing up at them, following in their trail. The rocks underfoot were loose and often gave way as I put my weight on them. In short order the ground raced up at forty-five degrees or more. Occasionally I put my hands down to aid my ascent, but it was more a case of putting my hands out to fend off the cliff.

I was gaining on the man ahead and presently he stopped for a rest and we paused to speak to him. It transpired that he and his wife were from a small town in Norway. We told him that we were from the north-east of England. We all agreed that the Yukon was a beautiful place and with that we carried on.

I enjoyed the physical challenge of the climb. My heart, lungs and legs were soon in a rhythm and I climbed like a machine, my mind empty of all except where to put my next footstep. The shade of the ridge had crept across me and the wind was gusting, the cold air stinging the sides of my throat. There was ice coating the rocks where water had seeped from the earth and snow patches became more frequent. A grouse leapt up shouting 'Go back, go back, go back', but I ignored its warning. I looked up to select the next part of the route. There were two options, one to the left and one to the right. Both options looked heinous, boulder strewn and icy. I decided to go right, but before I took my next step Gary called out to me from ten metres further down,

"Bob. I'm not going to the top. It's too risky with my arm, I've already just avoided putting it down several times."

"Okay."

"You go on if you want. I'll make my way onto the ridge there and take some photos and I'll wait for you to come down."

"Okay."

I looked up once more to where I had intended to go. It looked nasty. It was so steep now that I felt like I was about to start free climbing on a cliff. I felt daunted and seriously thought about jacking it in. It didn't look possible, and yet there was a lady in her fifties well above me. It was obviously possible.

I pressed on behind the Norwegian guy who had had a head start from our rest stop. The mountain became steeper and the ground more friable. Several times I scrambled for a toehold as the world lurched away from me. My heart was pounding with more than the exercise. The peak above was giddying and I dare not look back. If I did I felt I would see the precipice behind me and would feel myself being sucked backward like a photon before the event horizon of a black hole. What I felt now was less the challenge of a climb and more fear and the desire for it to be over.

I took a few more steps and slipped as a boulder rumbled out from under my foot. I momentarily scrabbled desperately for a new hold and then I stood up gasping for air. I was by now scared shitless, but I wasn't giving in with the Norwegians in front of me.

The snow patches suddenly coalesced into a continuous white blanket and to my great relief the loose boulders were buried. I was now kicking footsteps through the snow's crust to gain a better purchase. Above me the Norwegian lady had reached the summit and not far behind her, her husband stepped out from the shadow of the gully and into the sun. From the crest he shouted to me,

"Come on Newcastle!", knowing that I came from the northeast, and so presuming that I'd support Newcastle football club.

I'd set him right on that when I got to the top. I support Middlesbrough.

The view from the top, when I finally got there, back and armpits saturated in liquid fear, was magnificent. Mountains stretched off in all directions, their sides red and rust, their peaks white. Slightly to the left I looked up the wide valley of the North Klondike. The river itself glittered blue amongst a braided bed of grey gravel. I could see Tombstone, blued in the distant haze. Nearer, the car was a tiny speck of shiny metal an impossible distance below. Above, a series of white clouds rippled across the sky like the ridges in a ploughed field. To the right the road was a thread carelessly dropped on the landscape. It snaked its way beyond an unlikely azure lake in the distance where a purple-grey smudge of haze marred the lower portion of the sky. Behind me, where the ridge I was perched on plunged away, the mountains, if not for their caps of white, would have looked like the barren surface of the moon. I turned back to the North Klondike and just stared.

"Great view, huh?" the Norwegian guy said to me.

He had sat down on his rucksack on a patch of black scree beside his wife. He was slicing an apple with a penknife instinctively by feel as his eyes scanned the valley below. It was an action he had probably performed a hundred times on a hundred mountains. His breath danced away, a wispy sprite in the cold air.

"Fantastic," I concurred, the spell broken. "It was a bit scary coming up though."

"Yeah," he laughed. "I don't like heights. When I look down a cliff I feel it in my balls."

I smiled and nodded. I knew exactly what he meant, although I had felt the fear as a queasy feeling in my stomach. Now that I had reached the top in one piece my thighs felt slightly twitchy as the adrenaline wore off. I shakily sat down and put my fleece on and had a swig from my water bottle. I remembered his shout of encouragement.

"I support Middlesbrough football club," I said.

"Ahh," he nodded.

"We used to have a Norwegian play for us called Jan Aage Fjortoft."

The man's wife said something in Norwegian in the singsong phrases of the Scandinavian languages, obviously asking what I had said, as his reply included the name 'Jan Aage Fjortoft.'

He turned back to me and said,

"He's retired now. He works on TV, talking. He's not very good."

Football; what a great game. There is something primitive, tribal perhaps, about watching a game live in a stadium. Melanie and I have season tickets at the Boro and we sit amongst a crowd of nearly 30,000 others of like mind. For big games the atmosphere builds before the kick-off and as the players run onto the pitch there is a huge roar and blaring music. The hair on my arms and neck rises up and I feel emotion well up in my chest and throat. Its the 'Pride and the Passion' of football.

Nowadays, games are watched by the fans, by and large, in good spirit and the chants and songs and banter between opposing supporters can quite often be amusing.

"How do they know what to sing?" Lorna, a friend of mine once asked.

It's a good question I have thought about myself. I think perhaps one person comes up with a chant and shouts it out. That is clearly heard by say, the people in a twenty seat radius, which is 1600 supporters. If most of them then repeat it then by the next chorus the whole ground can hear it and join in. From the other end of the ground where you couldn't hear the first voice it sounds as if everyone in unison thought up a new chant.

I remember the Arsenal fans singing to us 'Shall we sing a song for you?' as they were panning us about five-nil and we had been stunned into silence. A guy near me yelled back,

"Go on then. How about 'Suspicious minds'".

In a recent game in the Premiership between Norwich and Manchester City, Norwich had gone two-nil up early on and then by half time had squandered their advantage. Their fans, with their team in the relegation zone, had slipped into a silent gloom. During the break Delia Smith, the TV cook and major shareholder of the club, came out onto the pitch with a microphone to whip up the fans' ardour. She told them that the team needed a twelfth man and she asked them 'Where are you?' The Manchester City fans responded in the second half with a chorus of 'There's only one Jamie Oliver'. Football fans are the unrecognized masters of quick wit and repartee.

I went to Austria in February 2005 to see Boro play Graz in the UEFA cup competition. We scored first and our section of the ground went mental. It's an amazing feeling when your team scores. I get goose bumps watching goals in slow motion on the TV on programmes like 'Match of the Day', because as the ball goes into the net you see in the stands behind the goal everybody's hands shoot into the air and they leap to their feet in unison. I can feel the emotion from my living room. Complete strangers will dance about and hug each other and all the normal rules of personal space and etiquette are forgotten in an instant of delirium. The Graz fans were silenced by our opening goal and we sang 'You only sing when you're skiing, sing when you're skiing, you only sing when you're skiing'.

I have supported Middlesbrough since my dad took me to my first game when I was about twelve. I am very lucky to support Boro at this particular point in time because we are at our most successful period in the club's history. I have followed the team to five cup finals. There have been Boro fans who have lived and died and never had the opportunity to go to a final at all.

I remember the Coca-Cola cup final in 1997. Over 30,000 Boro fans had deserted Teesside to make the pilgrimage to Wembley. I stood near a gate to the ground and looked back. Behind me was a concourse and it looked as if all 30,000 red shirted fans were coming over it. There was a massive red tide of humanity surging up to the ground. I felt part of something huge. We drew with Leicester that day; victory snatched from us by an equalizer in the dying minutes and we felt deflated on the long bus journey back. This was in the days before extra time and penalties and we faced a mid-week replay, which I was convinced we would lose. But I was cheered by overhearing a snatch of conversation behind me. A guy was talking on his mobile to a friend for a few minutes and when he finished he reported to his companion next to him,

"Steve says there were only lasses and dorks out in the Boro last night," I smiled wryly; the rest of us were at Wembley.

For the first time in 128 years we have finally won a cup. In February 2004 we went to the Millennium Stadium in Cardiff to watch the league cup final against Bolton. I will never forget it. The atmosphere there was outstanding. The roof over the pitch was closed and the noise of 75,000 fans was stupendous. We scored within the first two minutes and the Boro fans were in rapture. I yelled so much, I forgot to breathe in and felt faint. We were then awarded a penalty after five and a half minutes and I was delirious with joy. When Zenden banged in the penalty it was pandemonium in the Boro part of the crowd. We were in wonderland. It didn't go quite according to plan though when Bolton pulled one back and we had a long nervous wait until the final whistle. Oh, the rapture. There was singing, dancing and grown men in tears. That game had been our route into Europe and the resulting game in Graz.

Unbelievably, the 2005/6 season saw Middlesbrough in the UEFA Cup final in Eindhoven, Holland. We got there via two of the most outstanding games I will ever see. In both the second legs of the quarter and semi-finals, Boro found themselves conceding goals and needing to score four goals without reply to win. Both games were won in the dying seconds to send the fans into ecstatic delirium. Unfortunately, the final didn't live up to the buildup, but that's Boro.

At the top of Goldensides the Norwegian was telling me that the best ever Norwegian player was so-and-so (I can't remember his name).

"He played for a big English team. I can't remember their name," he said.

"Manchester united?" I prompted.

"No."

"Chelsea?"

"No"
"Arsenal?"
"No. They won a lot a few years ago."
"Liverpool?"
"No"
"Newcastle, Manchester City?"
"No. The managers son played in the team."
"Lampard? West Ham?"
"No."

I was stumped and so was he. Having seen the view and now feeling the cold at 6000feet on a sub-arctic mountain I decided to move. I bid my farewell and began my descent. Back in the shadows several hundred feet down I heard the cry,

"Nottingham Forest!" of course.

Perversely, I felt no fear whatsoever coming down the mountain even though the drop-off that I had been so terrified of even glimpsing during the ascent was laid out before me. I went down very quickly. In some places running, taking giant strides as the hill fell away beneath my feet. I was immune to the fear of crumbling rocks because as my foot landed, even if it slipped, I was airborne again for the next step. Every few minutes though I had to pause because the pressure in my thighs and knees was fantastic.

I overtook Gary, who was taking a sensible approach to the descent, which was only partly derived by the necessity of his arm. He told me when we arrived back at the car that, strangely to me, he had found the descent far more frightening and that the ascent had felt okay.

Chapter Ten

It was cold at Tombstone campsite. I was buried in my four-season sleeping bag, but I still felt it. I felt it even though I was wearing three pairs of socks, a T-shirt, a fleecy top, long johns, a woolly hat and gloves; in bed! It was light enough to see but I didn't want to withdraw my arm from my bag in order to check the time. The dilemma was whether to stay put and be nibbled by the chill with no hope of going back to sleep, or get up and move around. Getting up and moving around seems like the obvious solution to a rational mind, but it does involve getting out of a relatively warm sleeping bag and trying to get dressed in the hideous cold outside the tent. Shit. I wriggled in lieu of real movement, clamping the neck of my bag as I did so to prevent heat escaping.

"Gaz. Are you awake?"

"Yep."

"You cold?"

"Freezing my tits off."

"Shall we get up?"

"As long as you go first."

"How about we get up at the same time and just throw all our shit into the car and get going?"

"Sounds good," a pause. "Actually it sounds nasty, but it's better than lying here till we're dead. After three?"

"Okay."

"One, two, three."

And with that we went for a get-dressed-and-break-camp record. We didn't time it, but I'm sure we smashed all previous PBs. We were in the car with the heater on full blast at 7.15am. The temperature outside was a cool –11 centigrade.

It was to be our last morning on the Dempster Highway and although I knew our Yukon adventure was ending the sheer beauty of the drive prevented any melancholy thoughts from seeping in. I was athrill with the blue splendour of the gathering day, the vivid hues of the forest and the shapes of the hills. And there was always the chance of seeing another bear, a moose or a wolf.

After about thirteen kilometres we pulled into a gravel pit at a place called Grizzly Creek and the rest of the morning was spent hiking up a pass towards Grizzly Valley viewpoint. It was tough going requiring bushwhacking through dense birch and willow scrub and the view at the top was disappointing due to a dense haze. The trek back down to the car was a bit of a blur as I loped downwards following my feet. It was time to begin to make the transition back to civilization. The car took us, like a homing pigeon, back to its home in Dawson in time enough for us to catch our flight back to Whitehorse.

It was late afternoon when we were finally disgorged from the plane back at Whitehorse airport. We left the terminal building and walked out onto the verge of the Alaska Highway. It was roughly a mile-long plod to the end of the airport perimeter fence and I was sweating after only about a hundred yards. My back was loaded with my rucksack and I had my daypack across my chest, its straps slung over my shoulders on top of the straps of my ruck. My daypack had all my camera gear and other assorted essential stuff in it and it wasn't light. Gary was similarly loaded and by the look of him, similarly sweaty. How nice it would have been to toss all this gear into a canoe and let it do all the work. My boots sank into the sandy soil and threw up a billowing cloud of dust. It was so dry that I could easily see why forest fires were a problem here during the summer.

At the point where the perimeter fence made a right-angled turn the cliff at the edge of the bluff above town drew us inexorably towards its edge as if we were water to a plug-hole. We stopped some sixty metres above the town, resisting the downward pull long enough to admire Whitehorse spread out before us. I could see the river fringing the town in the distance and I could make out the yard of Kanoe People on the banks where we had rented our canoe, seemingly aeons ago. We rested for a few minutes letting the sweat evaporate from our T-shirts and then we gingerly negotiated the trail downwards. It was a knee-trembling descent over treacherously friable clay and sand, but we made it safely down onto Cook Street with a fairly minimal use of Anglo-Saxon. It was another long walk through the length of the town and out a further two kilometres upriver to the Robert Service Campground.

It felt good to be walking along the riverbank back to the familiarity of the campground. The swirling current of the Yukon gyrated immutably below us to our left and on the right, beyond the Robert Service Highway, was the huge clay cliff atop which sat the airport. A raven soared out from the trees along the ridge and called out a 'Craaaw-kronk' of encouragement. My feet picked up the tempo, no longer slogging through sucking sand but aided by the tarmac path.

Amongst the pines at the campsite we found an empty pitch by the river and I erected the tent and wrote an entry in my diary whilst Gary went for a shower. After I had had similar ablutions we headed back to town, blissfully minus rucksacks, to the Edge Bar and Grill where we ate massive burgers and chocolate cream pie swilled down with Kokanee beer.

I had taken the Alaska~Yukon Handbook with me to the bar so that we could decide what to do for our final day in Whitehorse before the flight home the day after that.

"It says here that an excellent day hike is to walk around Schwatka Lake and up to Miles Canyon, then cross the river on a suspension bridge and back on the opposite bank. What do you reckon?" I asked Gary, who dragged his eyes from the TV showing a world championship ice-hockey game long enough to say,

"Sounds good."

It was a crisp morning as we headed out for Miles Canyon. We had set off from the campground heading downstream towards town, but had then crossed the road-bridge and turned upstream towards the hydroelectric dam. The footpath wended its way amongst a mix of trees. The golden leaves of the numerous aspens fluttered in the breeze. The stems of aspen leaves are thin and flattened so that the mildest air movement causes the leaves to rustle. Some native North Americans refer to the aspen leaves as squaws' tongues because they are constantly in motion (how terribly sexist). It was a nice sound to accompany our walk.

The trail headed gently uphill past the hydro dam, which in 1959 had tamed the infamous Whitehorse rapids. The river still lashed and foamed within its channel as it was spat out from the dam and I could only guess at the fury of the water in the days of the Klondike goldrush. Looking at the mountains of water heaving and thrashing between the rocks I could not imagine a raft surviving it even in these relatively tame times. It must have been extremely harrowing trying to get one's gear down to Whitehorse a hundred years ago.

Many of the 25,000-plus stampeders who did try to shoot these rapids had never handled a boat before in their lives. They had managed to get their gear over the Chilkoot or White Passes, which had been, for 75,000 others, insurmountable and the end of the dream. In many cases the end of life. Perhaps emboldened by their feat so far, the survivors had built their boats and rafts on the shores of lakes

Lindeman and Bennett and as the warmth of spring released the river from its icy carapace they had drifted towards the rapids.

The first section of white water would have been at Miles Canyon where the river speeded up as it squeezed through this narrow defile. Then soon after it was onto the violently thrashing manes of the white horses that gave rise to the name of the town at their terminus. Several men were drowned in that aqueous maelstrom and many more lost their boats and all their kit.

In the face of the devastation the Mounties decided that some sort of intervention was needed before a lot more people were killed and so they instituted mandatory river guides. The craft of each stampeder was piloted through the rapids, the changeover to a river guide taking place at what was to become Canyon City. At the end of the rapids a tent city was born that would grow into modern day Whitehorse. Soon an eight-kilometre tramway was built from Canyon City to Whitehorse in order to carry the goods belonging to each craft and it was along the remains of this that we would walk once we had passed Schwatka Lake.

The sky had become vaguely threatening, darkening to gunmetal grey as we made our way around the lake. The wind picked up and waves coursed across the surface in jostling crowds. An eagle watched us intently from high in a pine as its perch was rocked this way and that by the wind that was trying and failing to distract its laser eyes.

A Kwakiutl legend tells of how the eagle once had poor eyesight. However, because it could fly into high places, a chief had asked it to be a lookout and to keep watch for enemy canoes. The eagle wanted to help and it persuaded the slug, which had excellent eyesight, to temporarily trade eyes. When the eagle had finished its guard duty it refused to give the slug its eyes back and that is why the slug blunders around so slowly now.

The wind in the trees was now making enough noise to cover the sound of our walking and even though we were close to town I was wary of the possibility of encountering a bear. I wanted to shout or clap, but didn't so as not to scare the eagle.

At the head of the lake we picked up the route of the old tramway along Miles Canyon. The canyon walls climb some 15m above the river, which races through the gorge in a blue rush. Huge columns of basalt make up the canyon walls and each column is five or six sided and welded to its neighbours to form, what looks like, a petrified honeycomb. The basalt was released 8.5 million years ago by a volcanic vent near Golden Horn Mountain some eight kilometres to the south.

The river bulled its way through the canyon in silence, its waters heaving against its constraining walls. The pines shifting in the wind sighed as if to provide the soundtrack that the river was missing. Prior to the dam raising the water level the canyon was even more spectacular, being another 15metres deeper and the water was churned to a white frenzy before its climactic rush over Whitehorse rapids.

When we finally reached it, there was nothing left at Canyon City to indicate that there had ever been a settlement here. I poked amongst the fireweed, curious as to what I might see rusting or rotting back into the Yukon earth. After a few fruitless moments I followed Gary back downstream in the direction of the Lowe Suspension Bridge. This wooden footbridge was built in 1923 and even though its timbers were painted white it wasn't an incongruous sight amongst the pines. It delivered us safely to the left bank of the river where we walked back into Whitehorse.

On Main Street there is a statue. It's of a gold rush era prospector and his dog. Both man and dog are laden with rucksack and panniers and looking eagerly ahead. The inscription reads, 'This statue is dedicated to those who follow their dreams.' This struck a chord with me. Gary and I had followed our dreams out to the Yukon. Gary was following his to become a photographer and I was following mine to try to become a writer. I dream of returning to the Yukon wilderness.

Now that I am back at home, thoughts of the Yukon are never far away. I often daydream as I drink a cup of tea by the patio doors and watch the birch trees in my garden as they go through their annual costume change; from a naked black and white, to bright green, to darker green, to yellow and brown, and back to naked. As the trees mark the seasons, I watch them and I wonder, 'how cold is it in Dawson? Has spring break-up begun on the river? How warm is the summer? Are the mozzies bad? How are the bears doing and how is my white wolf?' I long to feel that tangible silence suddenly being broken by the 'kronk' of a raven.

What had I learned in the Yukon wilderness? I had confirmed that I had a good, reliable friend in Gary. I had already known that friendships are one of the most important things in a person's life. Friends are a source of fun and laughter, they can offer advice and guidance and tell you the truth you need, even if you don't want to hear it. They can offer comfort and support in times of need. Perhaps what I hadn't realized was how little I sometimes talk to my friends on important issues. I'm a bloke. I don't do feelings. Perhaps if I did I would have found out that Gary was feeling guilty about me doing all the paddling on the river, when I could have reassured him that I didn't mind at all. We had made good time on the water and I had just been glad that we were both alive in such a spectacular place; Melanie was right, (she always is) I should do more than just grunt.

The Teslin had revealed the selfish side of my nature. I now know that I am prone to being selfish and if someone else points it out in the future I won't make the mistake of ostentatiously denying it. I will probably benefit from knowing my weakness, even if I'm too selfish to do anything about it. We never found out if Gary had actually broken his arm or not, as by the time we got home the pain had eased to such a degree that he never bothered getting it checked out.

The Yukon Territory had also driven home to me my love of nature. I was in a constant state of awe in that landscape. But it's not just the big creatures that amaze me, such as the bears, the wolves and the eagles. I am also fascinated by the tiny animals. As I write it's April and I have just come in from the garden where I saw my first bumblebee of the year. So early in the season this will have been a queen bee that had over-wintered underground. She was now preparing for the coming summer and the task of building up a new colony.

If we humans ever notice an animal, it is usually a bird or a mammal, something big, cute, or something mammalian that we have some empathy with. Invertebrates like this bee are largely unnoticed and that is a shame because they are complex and wondrous creatures. It had been a cold morning and in the shadows there were still the remains of frost and yet this cold-blooded animal was flying when many other insects could barely walk.

In order to get going on such a morning bumblebees warm up by contracting their flight muscles. As they do this, the wings don't flap as the muscles for the upstroke and downstroke contract at the same time, but the bee appears to shiver just as we would. The growing heat is conserved by the bee's hairy coat.

Finally, when it's warm enough the bee takes to the air, but here in the wind it is subject to cooling and so the heat in the muscles is conserved by a special arrangement of the circulatory system. The bee's heart is in its abdomen and here the blood is relatively cool away from the flight muscles. As the blood is pumped, via an artery, towards the thorax, where all the work is being done, it has to pass through the insect's tiny 'waist', or petiole. As it goes through the petiole it runs very close against the vein bringing hot blood back from the flight muscles. As the hot blood meets the cold the heat is transferred into the incoming arterial blood in a counter-current exchange system. The laws of physics dictate that heat moves from the hot area to the cold until both areas are the same and a counter-current exchange makes use of this fact. The system ensures that the coldest blood coming in meets venous blood that has already given heat to the arterial blood, but it's still the warmer of the two and so heat is transferred over. By the time the arterial blood reaches the end of the petiole it is now warmed up, but its still cooler than the very hot blood just emerging from the flight muscles and so it picks up even more heat. In this way barely any heat is lost to the abdomen.

All well and good for getting going, but as flight continues, or if it's a hot summer day, the bee is in danger of getting too hot and so it must dump heat. Unfortunately, the blood must circulate via the petiole where cool blood can't get to the flight muscles because it's being heated up before it gets there by this efficient counter-current exchange. The only way to cut off this effect is to stop simultaneous circulation and to have venous blood flow first and then let the arterial blood flow out. To do this the bee makes use of its respiratory movements. As the bee breathes in by making its abdomen swell this sucks venous blood through the petiole. The blood is under such pressure that the vein expands crushing the adjacent artery and preventing the heat exchanger working. Then as the abdomen shrinks again it forces the arterial blood forward. The artery is now the vessel to swell, crushing the vein and again preventing the heat exchange. In this way heat is drawn from the thorax into the abdomen where it can be lost to the air.

So the bee has a very efficient way of regulating its temperature in flight, but how does it actually get airborne? A lot of insects such as grasshoppers, dragonflies and butterflies have relatively slow wing beats and each beat is the result of a muscle contraction, which is stimulated by a single nerve impulse. But smaller insects such as bees, flies and mosquitoes have wing beats at frequencies of between a hundred and a thousand beats per second. At these speeds nerve impulses aren't quick enough to trigger one beat, fade away and then for another one to trigger the next beat.

In order to work, the muscles need to be stimulated to twitch by something other than nerve impulses. The muscles for flight aren't even connected to the wings; they are attached to the wall of the thorax. There are two sets that are roughly equivalent to a vertical and a horizontal arrangement. The muscles' effect is to distort the shape of the thorax and because the twitch is only very short and only a small percentage of the muscles' overall length, it is very fast.

When the vertical muscles contract the thorax is distorted and springs into a new position with a click. This causes the horizontal muscles to be stretched, and in these fibrillar-type muscles it is the stretching that stimulates them to contract. As they do so the thorax again distorts, clicks back and stretches the vertical muscles which contract again. The wings, attached to the wall of this bouncing thorax, beat up and down. In this way the thorax oscillates and flight takes place even though the nerve pulses ordering the muscle movement are only arriving after as many as 40 wing beats have been made.

If you watch a bee and then ask yourself some questions such as how does it fly, regulate its temperature, feed itself, navigate, see, smell, sting, socialize etc. then the answers can be amazing. Without bees and insects like them, many of our food crops wouldn't be pollinated. They are important to us and they are fascinating creatures. There are millions of others invertebrates no less fascinating, but hidden from our curiosity by their size and unobtrusive nature. Perhaps we should make more effort to find them.

Paddling in the Yukon Territory and travelling the Dempster Highway was a magical and humbling experience, which I have tried to share in this book. The Yukon Territory is surely one of the most beautiful and wildest places on earth. But you don't need to go to the far side of the world to find beauty in nature, it is there all around you, though it is sometimes hidden by a mask of familiarity, or by being on a scale that we are not used to looking at. The humble bumblebee is a case in point. Surely outside your door is the Garden of Eden and paradise is here on earth if you only take the time to look for it.